I'M TRYING MY BEST?

Actions that leverage the power of persistence and positivity to overcome obstacles and unlock your potential.

Written and Illustrated by

CARL HATTLEY

LONDON * CAMBRIDGE * NEW YORK * SHARJAH

Copyright © Carl Hattley 2025

The right of Carl Hattley to be identified as author of this work has been asserted in accordance with section 77 and 78 of the Copyright, Designs and Patents Act 1988.

All rights reserved. No part of this publication may be reproduced, stored in a retrieval system, or transmitted in any form or by any means, electronic, mechanical, photocopying, recording, or otherwise, without the prior permission of the publishers.

Any person who commits any unauthorised act in relation to this publication may be liable to criminal prosecution and civil claims for damages.

A CIP catalogue record for this title is available from the British Library.

This book represents the author's present understanding, opinions, and research on the topics discussed. The views, interpretations, and conclusions expressed in this work do not necessarily represent the views of any organizations, institutions, or individuals mentioned within. While every effort has been made to verify the information contained herein, the author and publisher cannot assume responsibility for any errors, inaccuracies, or omissions.

ISBN 9781035857050 (Paperback)
ISBN 9781035857067 (ePub e-book)

www.austinmacauley.com

First Published 2025
Austin Macauley Publishers Ltd®
1 Canada Square
Canary Wharf
London
E14 5AA

Special thanks to Trang, Huong, Eric and Zina

for their advice, support and life-long companionship.

Dedicated to Rowan, Quinn and Olivia as they embark on their own adventures.

Safe travels and a journey that is full of surprise and delight.

CONTENTS

PHASE ONE: PREPARE TO EMBARK 6
Committing to growth and new experiences

PHASE TWO: DESTINATION 20
Deciding where to grow and explore

PHASE THREE: BEGIN THE JOURNEY 32
Arranging how to grow and access new opportunities

PHASE FOUR: ON THE WAY 44
Building momentum and making progress

PHASE FIVE: DISRUPTIONS 54
Overcoming obstacles

PHASE SIX: CANCELLATIONS 70
Adapting to setbacks

PHASE SEVEN: ARRIVAL 82
Finding value in the journey

PHASE EIGHT: WHAT NOW 92
Acclimatising to new circumstances

PHASE NINE: WHAT NEXT 102
Opportunities are everywhere

PHASE TEN: EXPERIENCE 108
New horizons and unlocked potential

PHASE ONE:
PREPARE TO EMBARK

―

Stimulating growth and adopting a Traveller Mindset to navigate towards change.

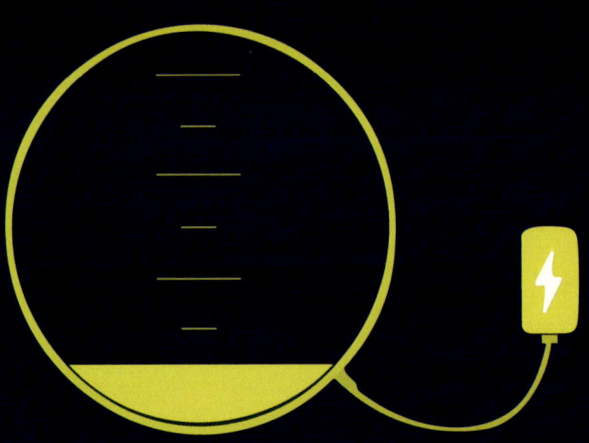

PREPARE TO EMBARK

Making changes or finding purpose is challenging, especially when figuring out what you want or where to go. Nobody will know your circumstances or motivations more than you. This book aims to help you recognise and leverage individual strengths and passions to drive meaningful changes that nurture personal growth and positive outcomes.

It's time to turn things around when feeling:

- Stuck, unable to move in any direction.
- Treading water, struggling to stay afloat.
- Trapped in a hole, unable to get out.
- Undervalued with nothing to offer.
- Adrift at sea, unsure which direction to paddle.
- On a rollercoaster with highs, lows, loops and spirals.

Growth can appear much easier for others. An example of this might be when looking for a new job. Some transition seamlessly from one job to the next, and then some face much rejection before landing a new job.

Comparing yourself to others can be demotivating and a source of anxiety. Those who appear to progress rapidly might have worked towards it for quite some time. They could also be lucky or in the right place at the right time. You might be making progress in other aspects of your life that others might be struggling with, and you are a source of admiration and envy for those people. Recognise and leverage where you experience **momentum** (ease) instead of **resistance** (difficulty). Elevate your strengths rather than place emphasis on perceived weaknesses to propel your growth journey.

This book aims to support:

- Progress towards goals that are already clearly defined.
- Identify meaningful growth opportunities when they aren't apparent.

GETTING STARTED

Growth opportunities

Adopting a temporary or practice goal is one way to start making improvements when it isn't clear what to do or where to begin. It can help lay the foundations for Change whilst helping to trigger something more meaningful. Consider exploring or working towards one of the growth opportunities listed below to get started or to tease out something more ideal.

- Career development
- Career change
- Lifestyle or quality of life
- Security and stability
- Sense of belonging
- Direction and purpose
- Unlocking potential
- Building relationships

Growth expectations

Whilst working towards a goal, it helps to **focus on the frequency and duration of time you can dedicate towards a goal rather than the desired outcome**; to avoid disappointment and frustration. For example, if the goal is to learn to play the guitar, then count every minute you can practice each day as a success, not the quality of your performance. Dreaming about the desired outcome can fuel motivation. However, finding ways to enjoy and value working towards the goal can help you stay on track when results aren't quick or easy to achieve.

Emphasising the time and effort you can dedicate towards a goal, rather than the desired outcome, can also help manage expectations and be open to opportunities. For example, when working towards career development, value the time you're able to spend each day preparing and improving yourself rather than a specific outcome, such as working at a particular company, so that you're receptive to unexpected opportunities for development and progression that might be more enjoyable or rewarding.

PHASE ONE: PREPARE TO EMBARK

STIMULATING GROWTH

Working towards personal development can be likened to planting seeds; not all will grow, but growth can occur in the right conditions. Similarly, personal development can also occur when nurtured in more advantageous circumstances.

1. **What you think (mental health)**
2. **What you're good at (skills and abilities)**
3. **What you enjoy (hobbies and interests)**
4. **How you spend your time (habits and routines)**
5. **How you feel (physical health)**

1. **What do you think (mental health)**

   Change can be a natural transition from where you are to where you want to be. Other times, it can be more disruptive and unsettling, where a cool head and steady nerves can help overcome complexities or uncertainties that arise when working towards personal growth.

   For example, when applying for a new job/promotion with a current employer, the fear of rejection might cause hesitation. On the other hand, applying for a job with a new employer can come with a fear of the unknown. The fear in either scenario might be overstated, casting a shadow over many likely positives. Perspective and your state of mind can alter how opportunities are perceived and have a discouraging or encouraging impact on making progress.

   Explore ways to gain a fresh perspective and make more informed decisions whilst fuelling the motivation required to navigate obstacles and have the confidence to act on opportunities.

   Some ideas to get started:
   - Share your kindness with others by finding ways to be helpful or volunteering in the local community.
   - Share positive experiences with family and friends to appreciate what you have.
   - Share coffee or tea with colleagues you rarely encounter to enhance your daily experience at work with new connections, conversations, and perspectives.
   - Share lunch with your favourite colleagues to appreciate each other's company in a different setting.

- Share responsibilities with others who are involved, impacted or benefit from a problem you're experiencing so that the world's weight isn't on your shoulders alone.

- Embrace a change of pace and take time out or a holiday to get some distance and space to reset, recharge and reflect on what's working and not working.

- Embrace a change of scenery for an alternative source of stimulation and inspiration. Try switching teams, visiting new places or spending time with different people.

- Embrace ways to overcome the debilitating impact of anxiety and stress. Try sharing your worries and fears with people who care about you, staying busy with a problem to solve, writing to clarify your thoughts, or allowing time to heal (like a cold or flu that comes as a surprise, disrupts the capacity to function for a while and then goes away after some time, leaving you more robust and more immune in future).

- Embrace influences that elevate you, and create distance from those that drag you down. Invest in yourself rather than make comparisons or seek the validation of others.

2. What you're good at (skills and abilities)

When in doubt, go with what you know and turn strengths into growth opportunities by doing more of what you're good at. Challenge yourself to master skills and abilities more profoundly or apply them differently to explore new possibilities or help others. Alternatively, expand your horizons by gaining new skills.

Recognise, appreciate and more frequently incorporate aspects of your personality that generate positive responses and outcomes. For instance, if being optimistic works well for you, look for more opportunities to be optimistic. The same applies to other traits such as being confident, curious, hard-working, helpful, open-minded, organised, patient, playful, or spontaneous.

Explore opportunities to broaden your horizons in ways that expand on your abilities and play to your strengths.

Some ideas to get started:

- If you're empathetic and a good listener, consider helping others by volunteering with phone services that supports older people and those in distress.

- If you're good with children or animals, explore events, activities or organisations you can contribute towards. Consider expanding your abilities more professionally, such as training as a vet, teacher, caregiver or entertainer.
- If you're talented in team sports or individual fitness activities, try joining a club or participating in an organised event (e.g. marathon).
- If you're confident and good at presenting in front of a crowd, try acting or dance classes.
- If you are handy around the home and garden, start a DIY project or fix something for a neighbour. Try expanding your abilities by learning practical skills like plumbing, woodwork or bricklaying.
- If you're a social butterfly, consider hosting more dinner parties and BBQs or becoming more involved in community, school or charity events.
- If you're a skilled worker, consider opportunities to pass on your experience as a mentor or trainer.
- If you're creative, find time to practice and improve your skills with others who share similar talents by joining relevant groups, clubs and events. Try painting, drawing, illustration, pottery, glass blowing or photography classes and groups.

3. What you enjoy (hobbies and interests)

Doing more of what makes you happy or adopting new interests and hobbies can help drive meaningful Change that you can be passionate about.

Joy can sometimes be the outcome of doing something less enjoyable, for instance, doing something tedious or mundane to make a loved one happy because their feelings are important. Or when a new job or promotion comes with less desirable responsibilities, but the salary increase might enable other benefits in your personal life that are worth the sacrifice.

Exploring new hobbies and interests can open the doors to new memories, skills, passions, professions, relationships and experiences.

Some ideas to get started:
- If you like to travel, learn a foreign language to stimulate the mind, impress relatives, or make travel more enjoyable.
- If you enjoy learning, enrol in a course or group that is mentally stimulating, like creative writing, history, philosophy or psychology.
- If you enjoy socialising, try a course or group that encourages interaction with others, such as dancing, acting, or various team sports.

- If you enjoy being handy around the home, try making time for more practical things such as gardening, beekeeping or woodworking.
- If you enjoy entertaining, try a course or class in something that makes an impression, such as cooking, magic, juggling, cocktail mixing or learning an instrument.
- If you enjoy being creative, try a course or group that encourages self-expression, such as painting, drawing, illustration, pottery, glass blowing, photography or sewing/knitting.
- If you enjoy nature, try spending more time in it. Picnic in parks, lounge on beaches, swim in lakes, boat in rivers, read with feet hanging over canals, wander in forests and camp in fields.
- If you enjoy reading in coffee shops, browsing shops, going to the cinema, relaxing in riverside pubs, exploring museums, and wandering markets, try doing it more often or whenever you feel like a boost.

4. How you spend your time (habits and routines)

Take control of your current situation by being accountable for your actions and choices. You have more time and power than you might realise when emotions obscure opportunities to invest in yourself. Innocent justifications like feeling too tired or busy can cause procrastination, where time is less productive and actions are less effective.

Even minor adjustments to daily habits and routines can add to significant changes like what time you wake up, what you put in your mouth, how you use the time when commuting to work and how you choose to unwind.

Be accountable, responsible and purposeful with what you do with your time by optimising personal habits and routines to be more efficient.

Some ideas to get started:
- Take control of what you do with your mouth, what goes in and what comes out.
- Take control of the time spent watching or browsing content on screens. Choose to do something less passive and more constructive with your time, or select content that might be more educational or productive towards your goals.
- Take control of your body and how often you move it by taking the stairs or walking whenever you can.
- Take control of your health when sitting at a desk for long periods by incorporating breathing, stretching and posture exercises whenever possible.

- Choose to complete mundane tasks you might often neglect, such as flossing or making the bed, because they raise your standards and help train the self-discipline required for more ambitious Change.

- Take control of the time you choose to spend on the couch versus exercising, walking or connecting with nature each day.

- Take control of when you wake up. Waking up earlier can create extra time for reflection and productivity.

- Take control of when you go to bed. Rather than snacking and watching television, consider an early night to be more beneficial.

- Take control of the time you choose to spend drinking alcohol when it limits your ability to be productive. You're potentially less likely to exercise or work towards your goal later that day and even less likely to wake up early the next day after consuming alcohol.

- Take control of your relationship with '**comfort food**' by thinking of it as '**celebration food**'. Rather than leaning on it to feel better after a long or painful day, have something to look forward to as a treat.

5. How you feel (physical health)

Maintaining a healthy lifestyle and improving physical abilities can increase performance and help you endure any hard work or extra effort required to progress towards your goals.

How and when you fuel your body can impact your ability to concentrate and be productive. Whilst exercise can help increase your ability to function at an increased capacity.

Physical activities can provide opportunities to elevate mood and refine motor skills and mind-body coordination that can help to build confidence in your physical abilities and visualise problems differently.

Rest, recovery, and maintaining good mobility and posture can help you stay healthy and in good condition so that you're in great shape to enjoy all the benefits of achieving your goals rather than being physically constrained due to neglect and wear and tear.

Some ideas to get started:

- Enhance how you fuel and power your body to stay energised, alert, attentive and in good shape. Intermittent fasting, calorie counting, drinking more water and substituting processed foods for foods without added ingredients complement my individual circumstances, but there are many options to research and consider.

PHASE ONE: PREPARE TO EMBARK

- Improve your strength and physical abilities to increase performance with activities that don't require much space and can easily integrate into a daily routine. Dumbbells, fitness bands, kettlebells and bodyweight exercises are flexible options, and 30-day challenges can be a way to initiate new habits with activities such as squats, pullups, push-ups, or planking.

- Enhance your stamina to increase performance towards your goals with cardio exercises such as jogging, cycling or walking outdoors. Minimal equipment or preparation is required and could complement a commute to work, social gatherings or shopping trips.

- Make improvements to flexibility and posture with stretching and mobility exercises while sitting at a desk or watching television to counterbalance the impact of those activities.

- Enhance your ability and readiness to be physically active and mentally alert by limiting alcohol, unhealthy food and getting plenty of sleep/rest.

- Enhance physical and mental recovery and ability to process events and emotions with enough time to rest and sleep. An early night after a lousy day might be more beneficial than prolonging and worsening it with late-night indulgencies, phone scrolling or streaming content all night.

- Participating in a sporting event can be a way to enhance confidence in your physical and mental abilities. Consider running a marathon, a charity hike or scaling a mountain such as the Three Peaks Challenge in the United Kingdom.

- Learning a new sport or physical activity can be a way to experience growth and reassurance that Change is possible when enough time and effort are applied to a suitable action. Activities like archery, skateboarding, martial arts, scuba diving, yoga, or skiing/snowboarding can create new possibilities to explore when travelling, opportunities to become an instructor or new ways to connect with others.

- Outdoor activities such as running, cycling, walking, fishing, and kayaking provide opportunities to connect with nature, open the senses and create space for reflection and inspiration.

- Spending time at a gym can help detach and take a break from working compulsively or excessively and be an alternative to habits and temptations at home that do not support physical health and wellbeing.

PHASE ONE: PREPARE TO EMBARK

TRAVELLER MINDSET

Growth and Change can come with growing pains and learning curves. Emotions can cloud focus and drain motivation. There's a temptation to go easy on yourself, treat yourself, and invent excuses and justifications for not doing what's necessary to make progress. Try to detach actions from your thoughts and feelings. If your goal is fitness related, go to the Gym when you don't feel like it. If your goal is diet related, have a healthy snack when you feel like an unhealthy one.

Progressing towards growth and change can feel like travelling to an unfamiliar destination. Both can seem exciting and nerve-racking. Both involve planning, preparation, and commitment. Both involve navigating obstacles, uncertainties and other people to arrive in unfamiliar territory where relatively simple tasks can become more challenging.

When considering growth opportunities, try to shake any anxiety or insecurities that might be present. Think of it as going on holiday somewhere new; adopt a traveller mindset as your growth journey explores new horizons, adventures and opportunities.

It takes time and effort to travel from one place to another. Some things can go wrong, and some things can go right. A lousy holiday experience doesn't necessarily mean you won't go on holiday again. Consider how a traveller mindset might help you shift your perspective as you embark towards your goals.

1. **Commit to going somewhere**
2. **Decide where to go**
3. **Begin the journey**
4. **On the way**
5. **Disruptions**
6. **Assistance**
7. **Cancellations**
8. **Scenic route**
9. **Arrive**
10. **Repeat**

1. Commit to going somewhere

Avoid putting off or delaying travelling (making progress) from one place to another and commit to going somewhere rather than nowhere. Side-step procrastination by starting small and committing to more practical changes that will cultivate the discipline required to follow through on more ambitious goals.

2. Decide where to go

Although it's tempting to stick to what's comfortable and familiar, new ideas, options, and opportunities are beyond the current situation. Begin travelling (making progress) towards something new that's easy to get to, then branch out further as you gain experience and build confidence.

3. Begin the journey

Once you've committed to a new destination, the next step is to make a start and get moving (make progress) towards that destination regardless of any demotivating thoughts and feelings that might be present. A small step or slow start is better than not starting at all. Be proactive and embrace whatever means of motion are within your control.

4. On the way

Travelling (making progress) towards something new might require unfamiliar methods or abilities. Gain momentum by leveraging repetition to master new behaviours and skills into new habits and routines so that travelling towards a goal becomes more familiar. For instance, a long flight is less intimidating once you've taken a short flight, and once you've learned to ride a bicycle, the emphasis is more on where you are going and less on how to ride a bicycle. A goal might seem out of reach because more practice is required before making progress can feel more intuitive and accessible.

PHASE ONE: PREPARE TO EMBARK

5. **Disruptions**

A delay whilst travelling (making progress) means the journey is ongoing and will take longer than anticipated, not that it is cancelled or impossible. Avoid delays by choosing more reliable options and maintaining a healthy balance between circumstances that give you a boost versus those that slow you down. Have patience and persistence when situations don't adapt well to change or when some paths you share with others diverge or grow apart for a while. Persevere when disruptions come between where you are and where you want to be. Disruptions are a common occurrence and often out of your control. Allow time for pathways to open or consider alternative ways to make progress.

6. **Assistance**

Travelling (making progress) from one place to another is a social activity. Even when you feel alone, others travel and live alongside and around you—welcome opportunities to support or align with others who have shared goals, circumstances or destinations. Embrace any fleeting, recurring or lasting moments of support, comfort and inspiration with those you encounter on the way.

7. **Cancellations**

When travelling (making progress) from one situation or place to another is cancelled, not all travel or progress is cancelled. Only that particular situation at that moment in time is cancelled. Failure and uncertainty are part of the process. Refrain from settling for less when plans don't work out. Reflect on what you've learned and apply it towards something more promising.

8. **Scenic route**

When travelling (making progress) towards somewhere new, celebrate the wins (especially the little ones) and enjoy any surprises, lessons learned, and moments experienced on the journey. Anticipation can sometimes obstruct appreciation of what is happening in the present moment. For instance, being preoccupied about where you're going on a train might distract from how beautiful the view is out the window. Find delight and joy in doing a task, in addition to the satisfaction of completing one.

9. Arrive

Congratulations, you've navigated time and space to progress towards a goal, new environment or situation. The destination may have changed, and the view might be better or less than expected. Explore!

10. Repeat

Where next?

What's the next challenge?

BON VOYAGE

Your journey might be near or far, turbulent or tranquil, exhilarating or tedious. You may feel lost, sidetracked, or take several detours before arriving at your destination. The methods and techniques in this book aspire to help navigate uncertainty and ambiguity by defining clearer direction and purpose while providing comfort, hope and reassurance along the way.

Safe travels. I can't wait to hear all about it.

PHASE TWO: DESTINATION

PHASE TWO:
DESTINATION
———

Feeling in-between, neither here nor there.

Looking for inspiration before knowing where to start and how to begin.

PHASE TWO: DESTINATION

Questions to help frame problems and gain perspective.
___

PHASE TWO: DESTINATION

FEELING OUT OF PLACE

You can fit in but belong somewhere else.

What might help?
    a. Suppress the feeling and don't change anything?
    b. Change yourself?
    c. Change your environment?

PHASE TWO: DESTINATION

FEELING TRAPPED

Focus on what's within your control when unable to escape the current situation.

What might help?
   a. Speed up?
   b. Slow down?
   c. Stop or pause?
   d. Give up?

PHASE TWO: DESTINATION

RESPONSIBILITIES

Responsibilities or the fear of failure and uncertainty with the unknown can come with an uncomfortable level of risk that holds you back.

What might help?
    a. Don't change anything?
    b. Share the load?
    c. Reduce, optimise or consolidate the load?
    d. Expand or enhance your capacity?
    e. An alternative solution?

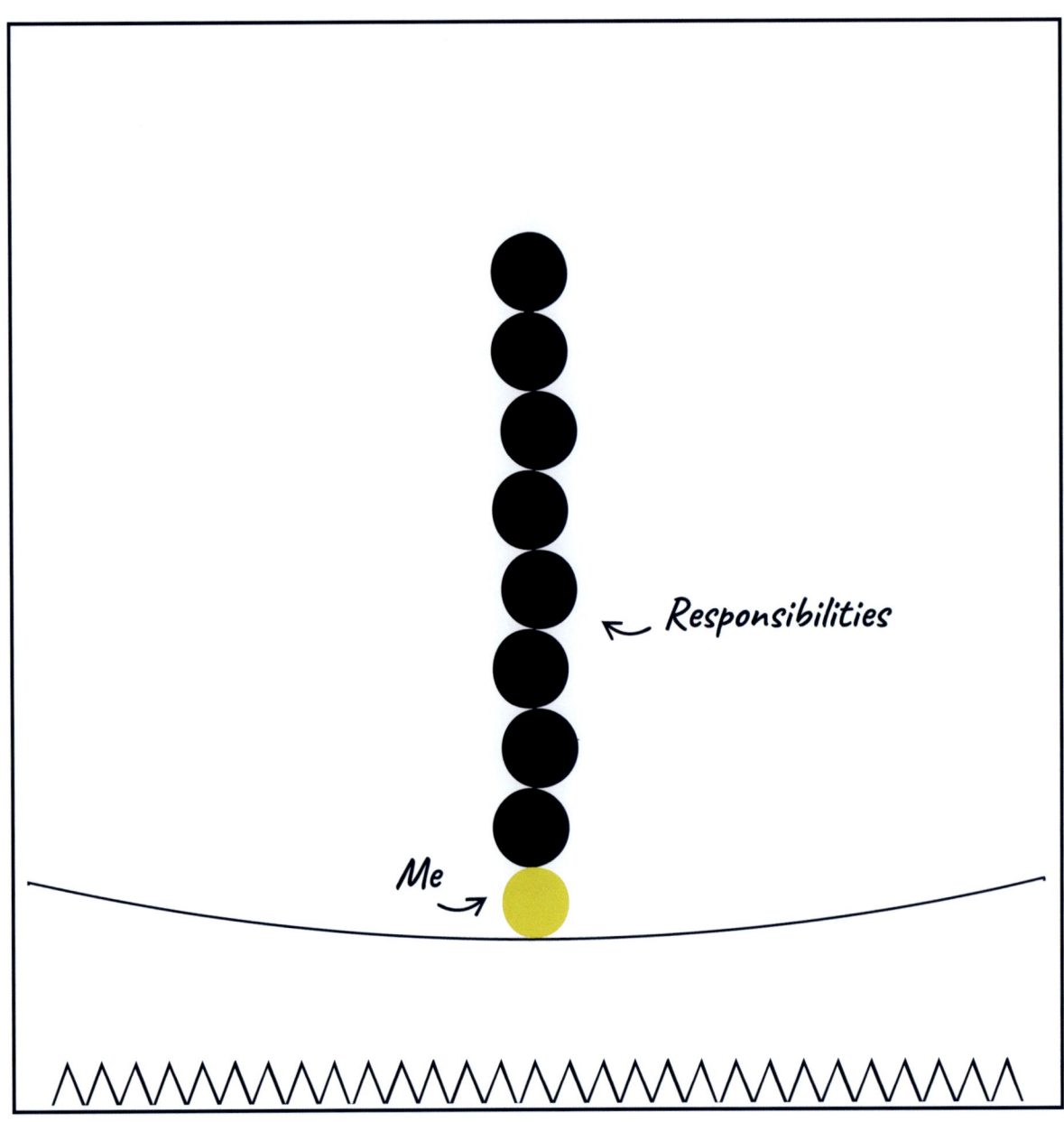

PHASE TWO: DESTINATION

FEELING SMALL

Feeling inadequate or unequipped for the challenge ahead.

What might help
a. Give up?
b. Share the challenge?
c. Break it down into smaller challenges?
d. Expand or enhance your capacity?
e. Try a different challenge?

A combination of options might be applied when training for a challenge like a Marathon. Firstly, it helps to have a training buddy or supporters to share the challenge with, whilst training incorporates smaller runs that gradually build up to more extensive runs.

PHASE TWO: DESTINATION

TRANSITION

Moving from one place or situation to another and feeling like a fish out of water.

What might help?
    a.   Ignore the feeling and carry on?
    b.   Share the transition?
    c.   Break it down into smaller changes?
    d.   Expand or enhance your capacity?
    e.   Give up?

PHASE TWO: DESTINATION

Activities to help find inspiration and motivation.
———

Negative

> ~~Something is **missing** or **out** of place.~~

Positive

> *Something needs to be **added** or put **in** the right place.*

PHASE TWO: DESTINATION

MISSION ~~(IMPOSSIBLE)~~ POSSIBLE

ACTIVITY 2.1

Reflect on previous occurrences when you've achieved something unexpected or unlikely. You might have put it down to luck, chance or fate. However, you probably did something to enable the situation.

Remember that you can do great things. You've done it before, and you can do it again.

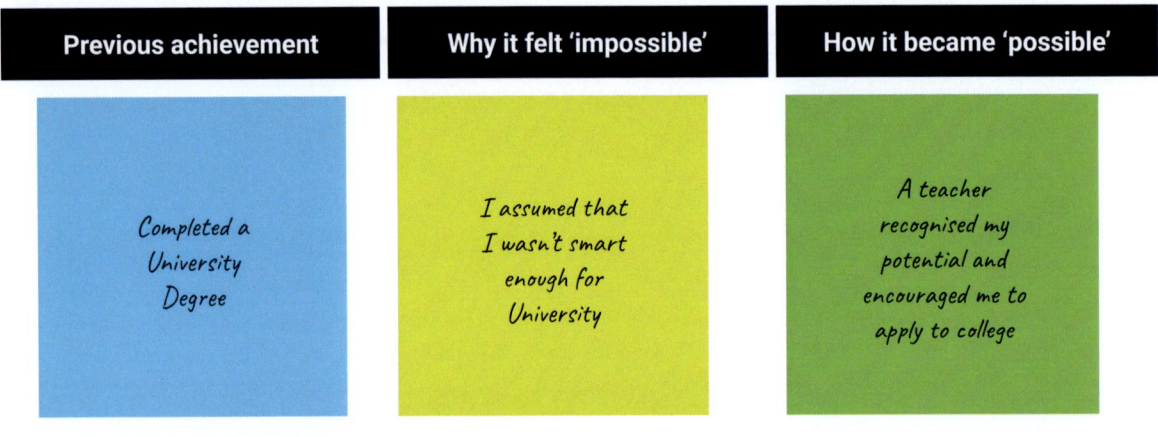

Try sticky notes on a wall or a spreadsheet

Previous achievement	Why it felt 'impossible'	How it became 'possible'
Ran the London Marathon	Marathons are for athletes, not me and my weak knees	Inspired and encouraged by work colleagues

PHASE TWO: DESTINATION

PERFECT DAY AT WORK

ACTIVITY 2.2

Imagine the perfect day at work. What would happen, and how would you like to spend your time?

The activity below might help identify opportunities to be more purposeful and accountable for your experience at work.

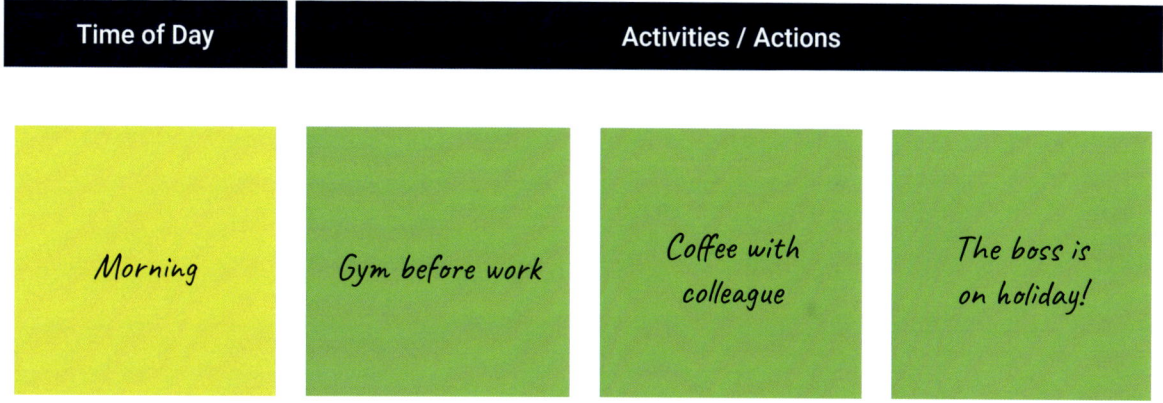

Try _sticky notes_ on a wall or a _spreadsheet_

Time of day	Activities / Actions
Morning (6am - 12pm)	*A productive morning without distractions*
Lunch	*Take a break from the screen and walk for 30mins*
Afternoon (12pm - 5pm)	*Get recognition for something going well*
Evening (5pm - 8pm)	*Get home earlier than usual*
Dinner	*Eat something healthy with family or friends*
Night (8pm -6am)	*Sleep well and fall asleep without thinking about work*

PHASE TWO: DESTINATION

THE PERFECT DAY OFF

ACTIVITY 2.3

Imagine the perfect day off. What would happen, and how would you like to spend your time?

The activity below might help identify opportunities to be more purposeful and accountable for your experience outside of work.

Time of Day	Activities / Actions

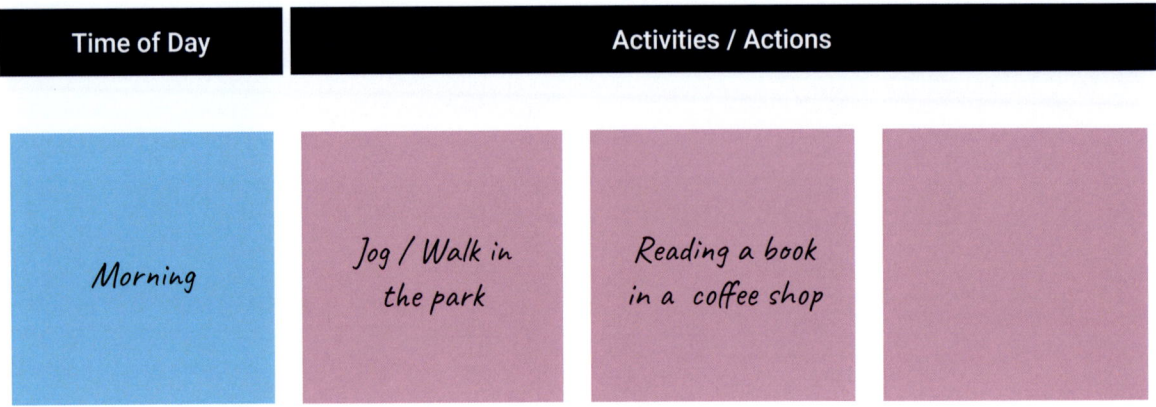

Try sticky notes on a wall or a spreadsheet

Time of day	Activities
Morning (6am - 12pm)	Exploring museums or wandering markets
Lunch	Relaxing in a riverside pub with a science fiction novel
Afternoon (12pm - 5pm)	Being creative or learning a new skill
Evening (5pm - 8pm)	Arts and crafts with the children and reading bedtime stories
Dinner	Eat something fun with family or friends
Night (8pm - 6am)	Movie or game night with family

PHASE TWO: DESTINATION

REFLECTION

ACTIVITY 2.4

Think about the people, activities, and places that inspire or motivate you.

Reflect on what you are thankful for and what you would like to change to help identify what's essential and highlight strengths to develop and opportunities to explore.

What are you thankful for?	What would you like to change?
My Job *Salary & Work/Life Balance*	*My Job* *Spice things up by taking on a new challenge*

Try sticky notes on a wall or a spreadsheet

Question	Answer
What are you thankful for?	
What would you like to change?	
What do you enjoy?	
What makes you mad or sad?	
What are you good at?	
What aren't you good at?	

31

PHASE THREE: BEGIN THE JOURNEY

Travelling from one place or situation to another will likely take time and effort. However, not knowing where to go and how to get there can make starting difficult.

Get moving! Moving (in any direction) can help inform or clarify the path ahead.

- A single step (action) could turn into a leap (an achievement) or a stumble (learning).
- A single step might lead to more steps (progress).
- A single step might also go nowhere or back to where you started (having gained experience).

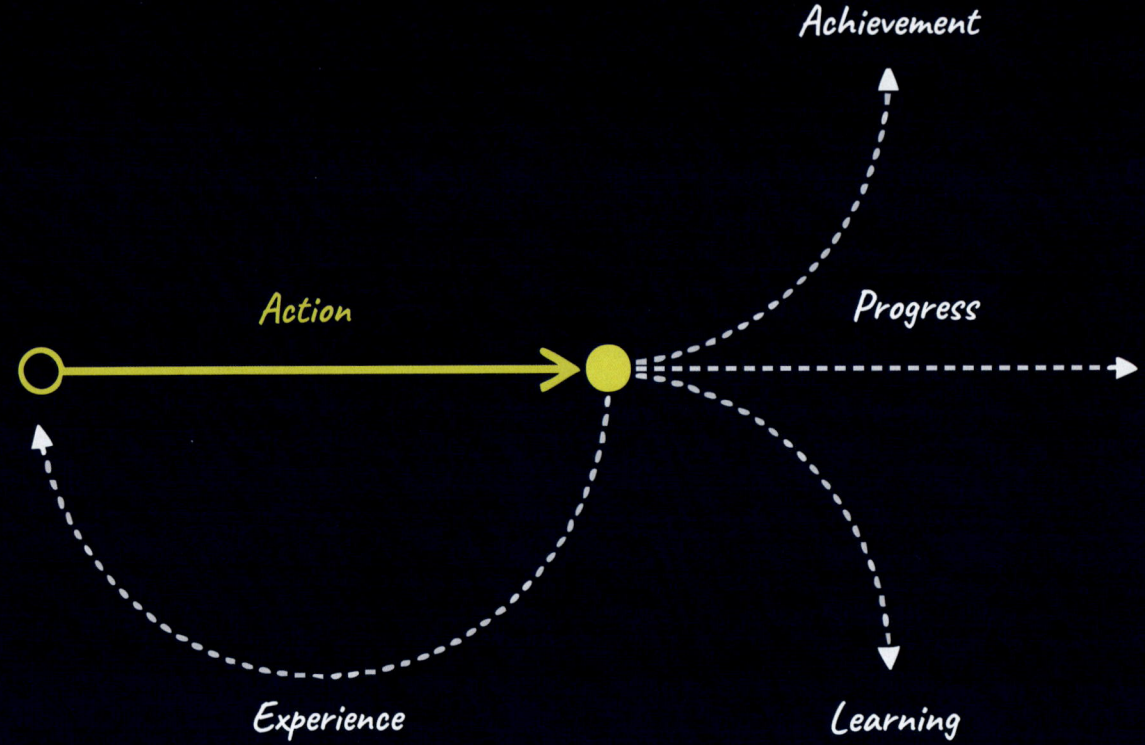

PHASE THREE: BEGIN THE JOURNEY

Questions to help frame problems and gain perspective.
———

PHASE THREE: BEGIN THE JOURNEY

LOOKING AHEAD

Picture yourself five years from now; what would you like to see?

What might help?
    a. Everything is the same?
    b. New or improved skills?
    c. New or improved home?
    d. New or improved job?
    e. New or improved relationships?
    f. Something else?

PHASE THREE: BEGIN THE JOURNEY

PRIORITIES

It's easier to boil water in a pan than it is to boil water in a lake. Focus on thoughts, actions or activities that are most effective to drive momentum.

What might help?
 a. Make a list of goals, problems, or tasks and try to focus on one thing at a time?
 b. Only move on to the next thing when the current task or focus area has progressed, resolved or paused?
 c. Take on everything and attempt to please everyone all at the same time?

PHASE THREE: BEGIN THE JOURNEY

SEIZE THE DAY

Trust your instincts, take control and follow through on opportunities to move forward and make progress.

What might help?
  a. I'll get to it later?
  b. It'll probably never work?
  c. I'm still getting ready?
  d. I don't have time?
  e. I'll give it a go?
  f. I'll make a start and do what I can?

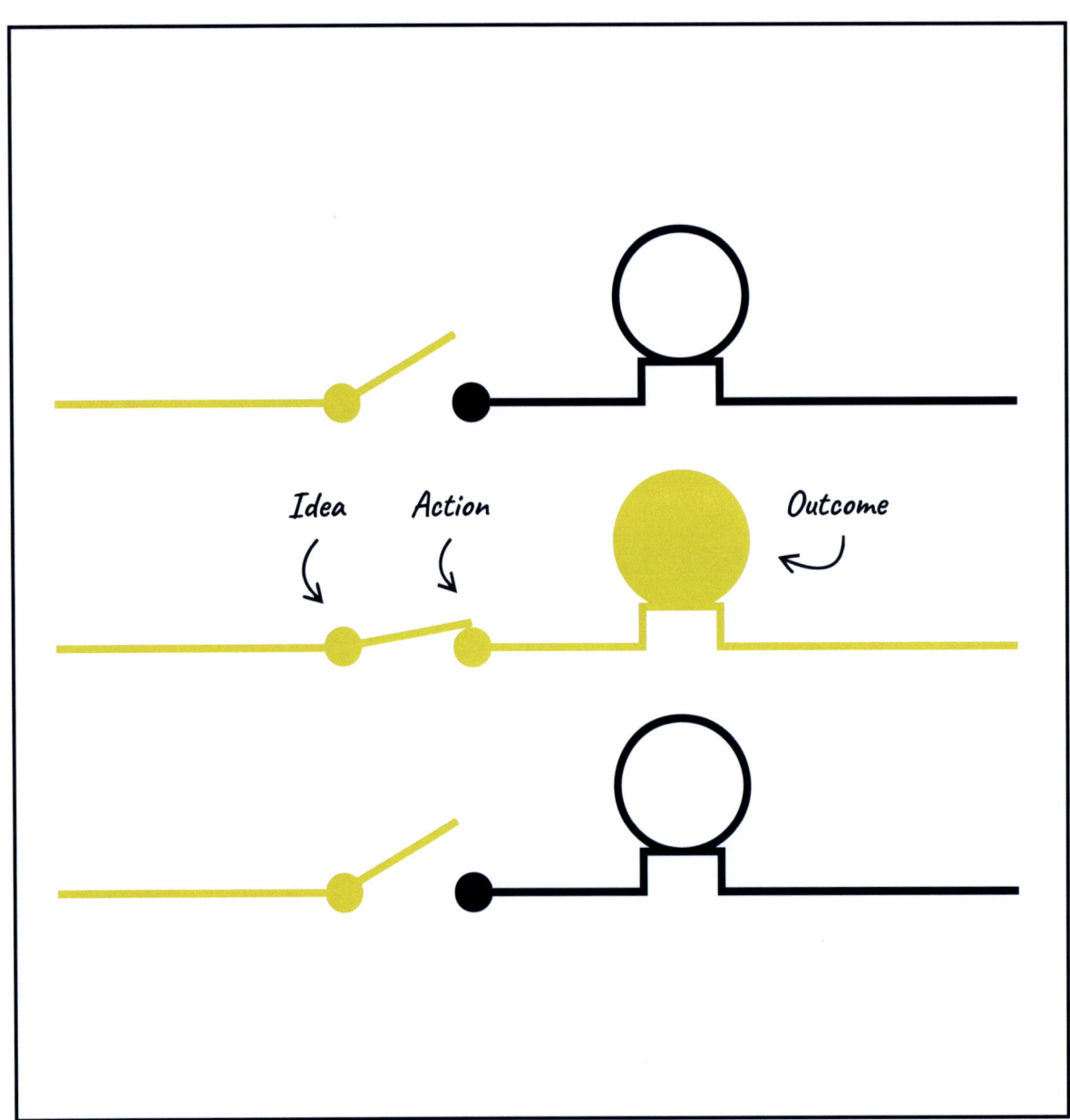

PHASE THREE: BEGIN THE JOURNEY

Activities to help find focus and direction.

―

Negative

~~*Nothing plus* **nothing** *equals nothing.*~~

Positive

Nothing plus **one**, *equals something.*

PHASE THREE: BEGIN THE JOURNEY

GROWTH AREA

ACTIVITY 3.1

Reflect on what's essential and consider what aspects of your current situation you want to focus on and improve.

Identify 1-3 focus areas from the list below or create some of your own in a list on your phone, on paper or with _sticky notes_ on a wall.

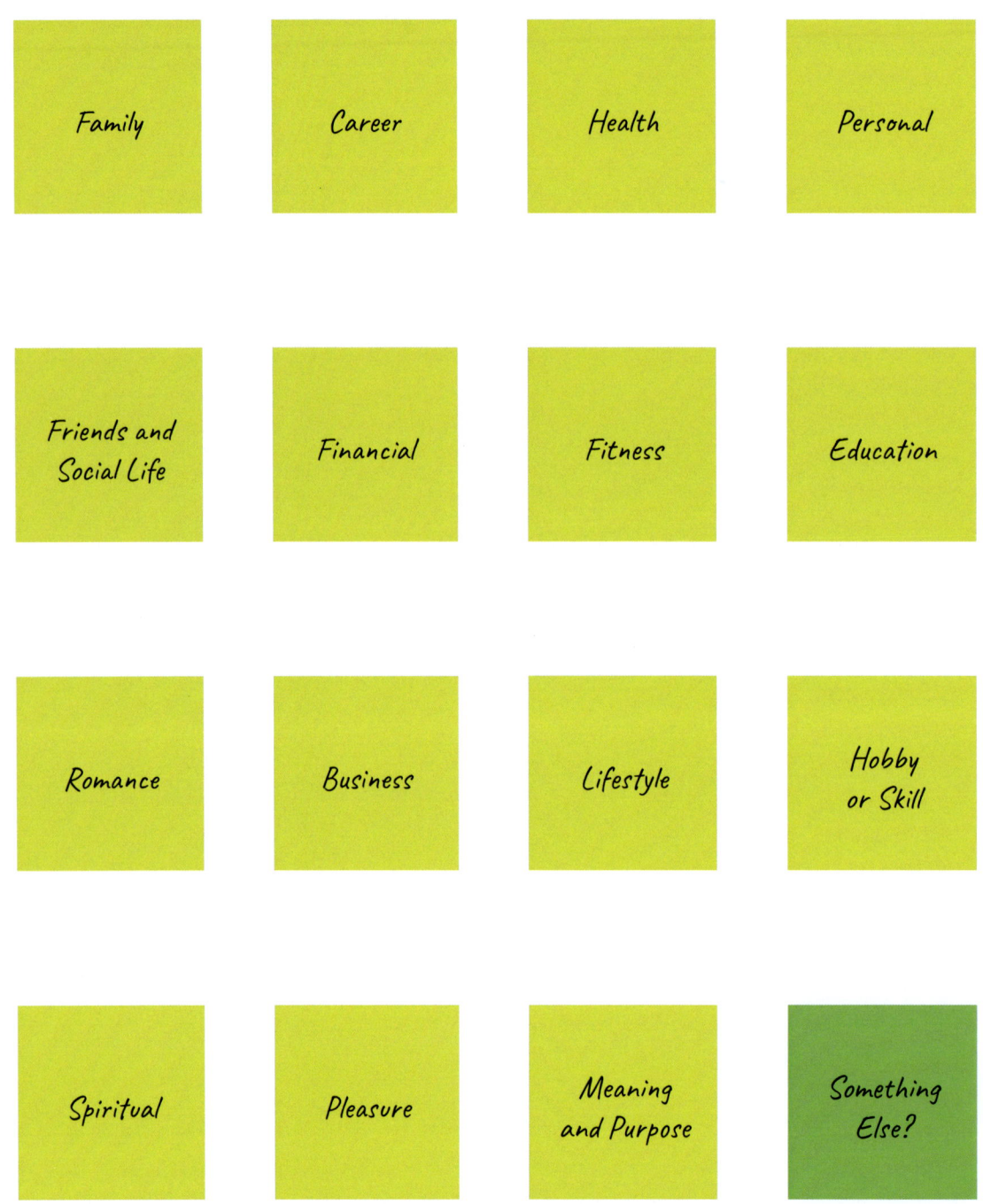

PHASE THREE: BEGIN THE JOURNEY

OPPORTUNITIES

ACTIVITY 3.2

Once you've identified some areas to focus on, consider what changes or improvements you would like to make in each area of focus.

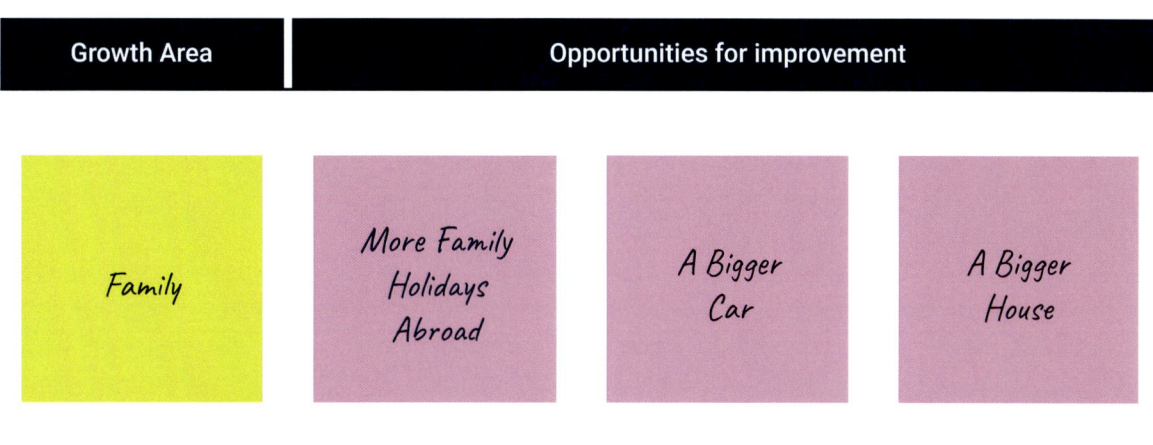

Try sticky notes on a wall or a spreadsheet

Growth Area	Opportunities for Improvement
Career	Become an Author
Family	More family holidays abroad

PHASE THREE: BEGIN THE JOURNEY

CHALLENGES

ACTIVITY 3.3

Reflect on what prevents you from making the changes or improvements you would like to make in each area of focus.

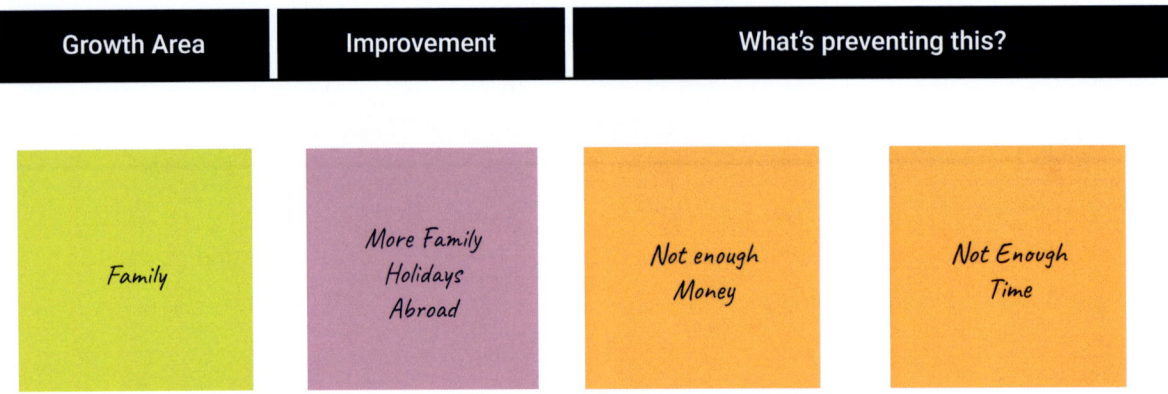

Try sticky notes on a wall or a spreadsheet

Growth Area	Improvement	What's preventing this?
Career	Become an Author	Not enough time or inspiration.

PHASE THREE: BEGIN THE JOURNEY

ENABLERS

ACTIVITY 3.4

Consider what is within your control and what actions are within your grasp to help you progress with the changes or improvements you would like.

Growth Area	Improvement	What's preventing this?	
Family	More Family Holidays Abroad	Save by spending less on takeaways	Over spending on Christmas and Birthdays

Try sticky notes on a wall or a spreadsheet

Growth Area	Improvement	What (action) might help?
Career	Become an Author	Dedicate 30 minutes every day during lunch to researching and writing

PHASE THREE: BEGIN THE JOURNEY

TARGETS

ACTIVITY 3.5

Once you have decided on a goal, plan when you want to see results and what you can do to make it happen.

Month	Goal	Commitment
January	Save £200 each month towards family holiday.	Reduce spending on takeaways and coffee.
February		
March		
April	Feel better about work	Had coffee with 3 colleagues I admire to learn more about their work and approach to work.
May		
June	Learn basic greetings in Vietnamese	Practice 20 minutes each day on the commute to work
July		
August		
September		
October		
November		
December		

PHASE THREE: BEGIN THE JOURNEY

COMMITMENTS

ACTIVITY 3.6

Once you've decided on a goal and when you want to see results, commit to actions or habits you can introduce to your routine that will ensure success.

Keep track of the commitments you have made so that you can visualise your progress and identify any room for improvement.

Below are examples of how you might track opportunities to save money. This technique could also apply to opportunities to practice a new skill, exercise, submit job applications or other recurring commitments that can support a goal.

Month						
1 *Begin goal to save money*	2	3	4	5 *Didn't spend on takeaway (Saved £60)* ✓		
8	9	10 *Spend less on Coffee (Spent £10)* ✗	11	12 *Didn't spend on takeaway (Saved £60)* ✓		
15	16	17	18	19 *Spend less on takeaway (Spent £60)* ✗		
22	23	24 *Spend less on Coffee (Saved £10)* ✓	25	26 *Spend less on takeaway (Saved £20)* ✓	27	28 *Review progress of goal to save money* *+ £100* *- £70*

PHASE FOUR:
ON THE WAY

You've chosen a direction and a way to advance from your current place or situation to somewhere more interesting.

You've already made progress by believing in yourself, putting yourself out there, and taking steps to improve your situation. It can feel unsettling, but you're on the way to progressing from where you are to where you want to be.

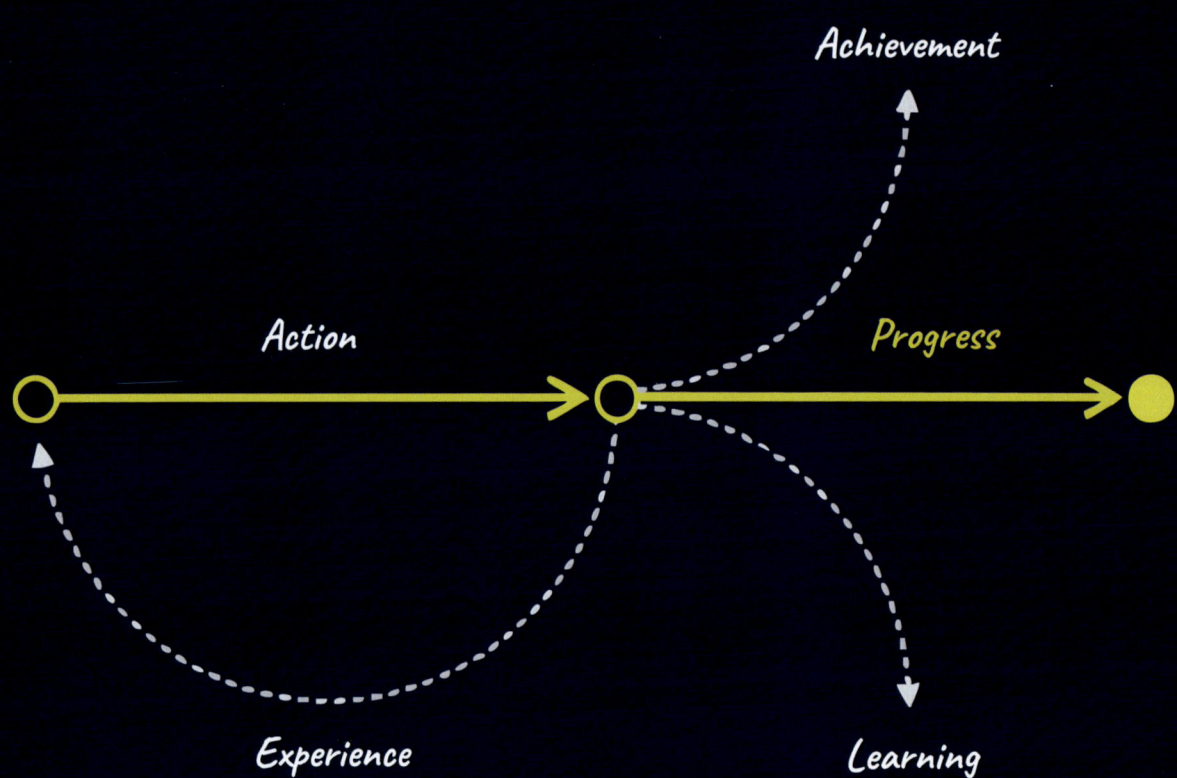

PHASE FOUR: ON THE WAY

Questions to help frame problems and gain perspective.
___

PHASE FOUR: ON THE WAY

PRACTICE

Small changes add up over time. Leverage consistency or repetition by introducing subtle changes in your daily routine to nurture growth progressively.

What might help?
    a. Add 20 minutes of exercise to your daily routine?
    b. Stop something unproductive in your daily routine?
    c. Reduce something unhealthy in your daily routine?
    d. Practice a skill for 20 minutes every day?
    e. Save a little every day and watch it grow over time?
    f. Something else?

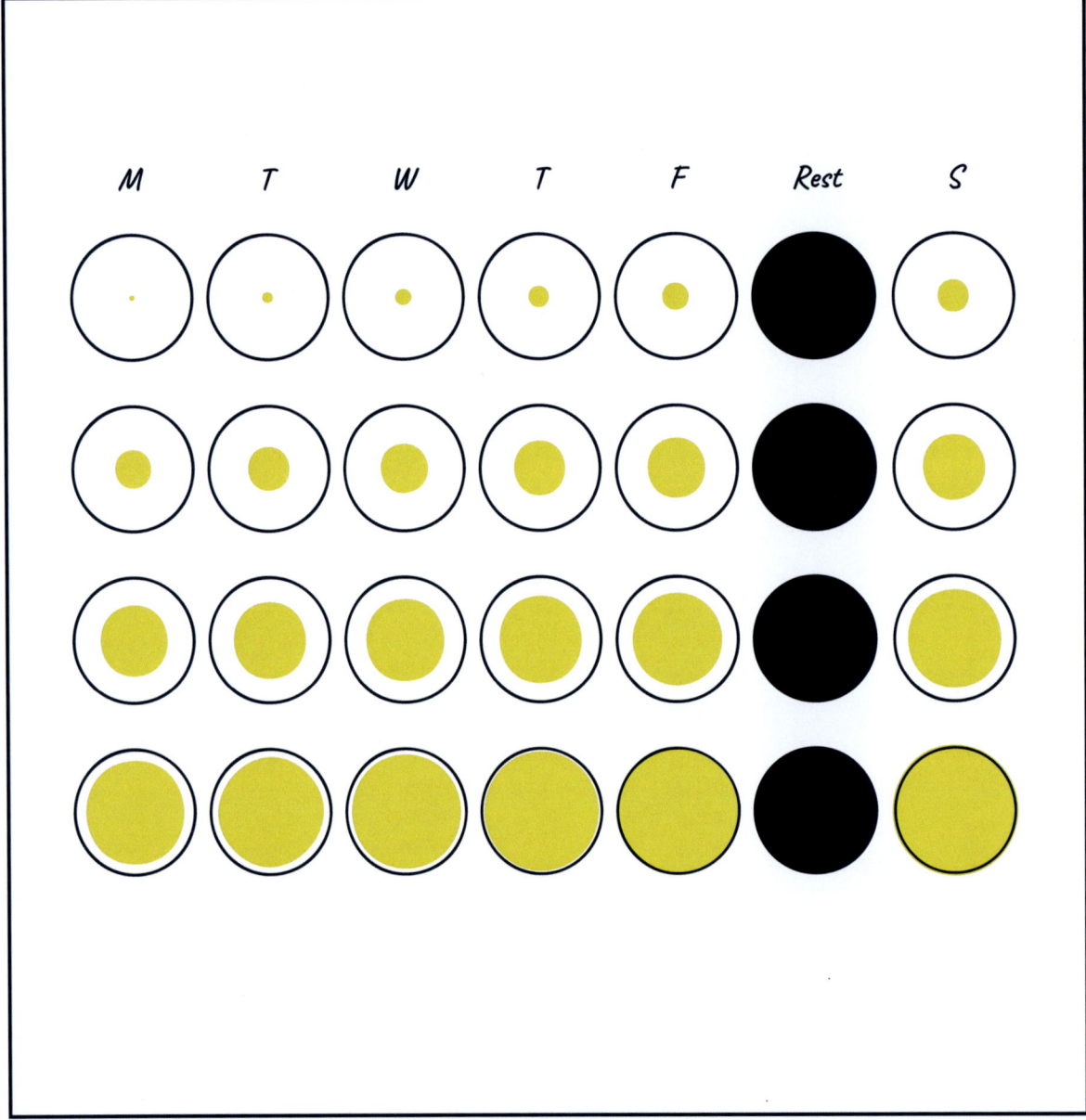

PHASE FOUR: ON THE WAY

FOCUS

Stay focused on what's most important by limiting the influence of distractions.

What might help?
    a. Focus on what makes you happy or what helps with your goals?
    b. Focus on your duties and responsibilities?
    c. Live in the moment and focus on whatever pops up?
    d. Focus on what other people tell you to focus on?
    e. Focus on what upsets you?
    f. Focus on what's out of your control, like the past, future or behaviour of others?
    g. Focus on everything?

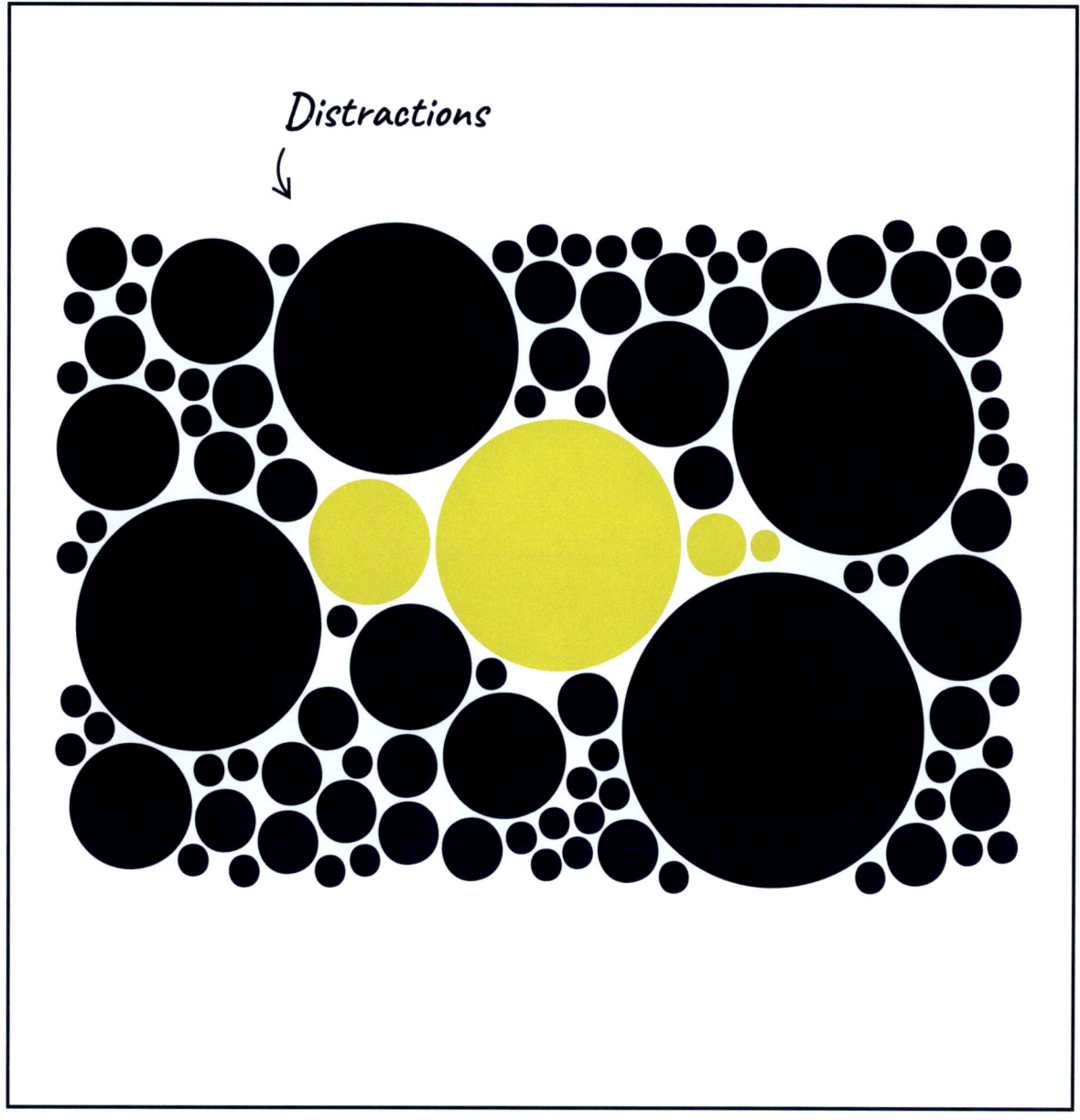

PHASE FOUR: ON THE WAY

TRY YOUR LUCK

You have what it takes to succeed; sometimes, it's down to luck or being at the right time and place.

What might help?
  a. A chance to succeed is more promising than no chance to succeed?
  b. You've surprised yourself before, and you can do it again?
  c. Succeed or fail, You'll learn something about yourself, such as what you value and what you might improve?
  d. There's no point in trying because you'll never succeed?
  e. It might not work out this time, but you'll have fun trying?

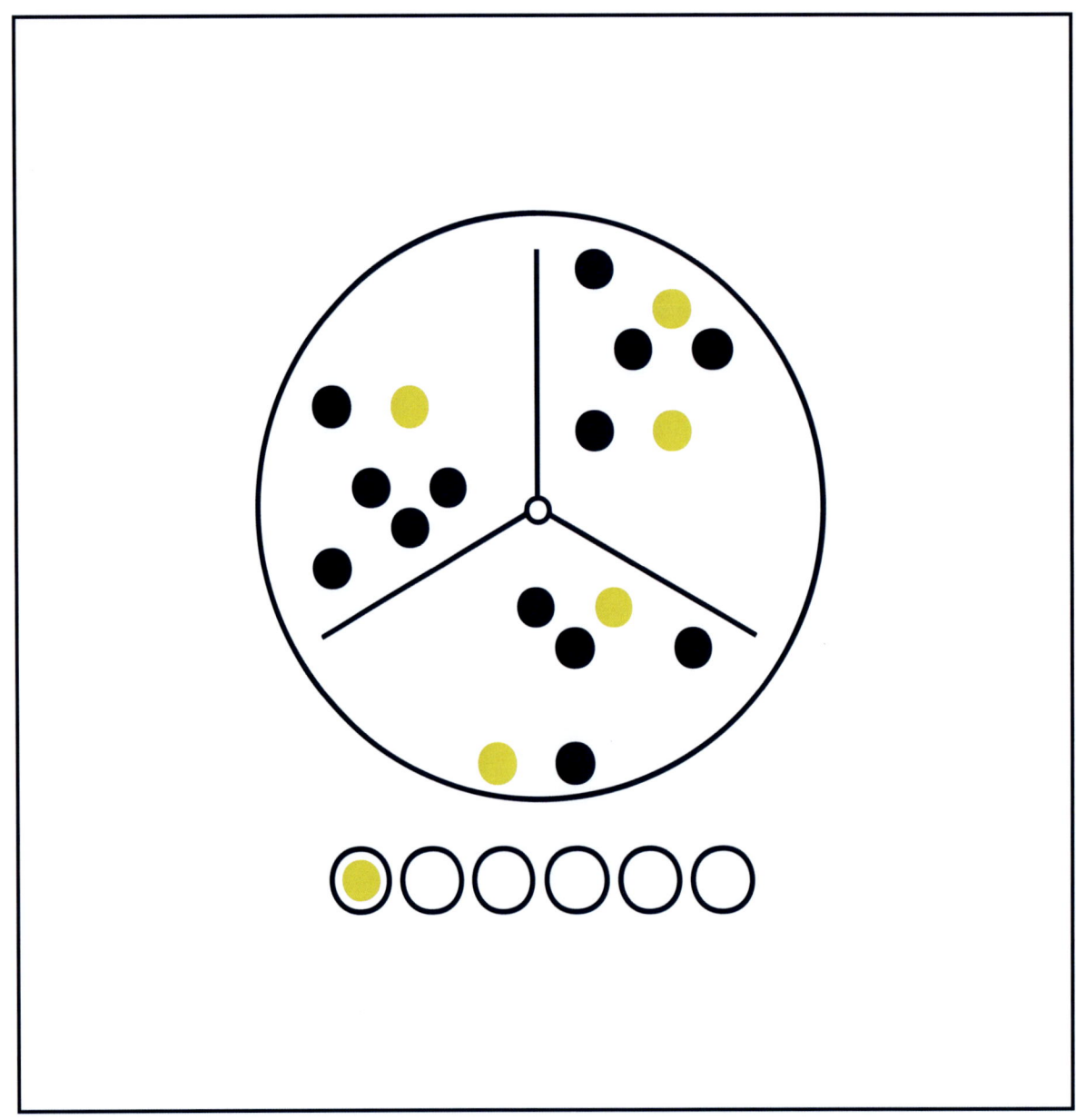

48

PHASE FOUR: ON THE WAY

Activities to help drive momentum and make progress.
―

Negative

> ~~A path with resistance can feel **daunting**, like climbing a mountain.~~
>
> ~~A path without resistance can feel like **slipping** on ice.~~

Positive

> A path with resistance can feel **rewarding**, like climbing a mountain.
>
> A path without resistance can feel like **gliding** on ice.

PHASE FOUR: ON THE WAY

OPTIMISE THE DAY

ACTIVITY 4.1

Reflect on the time you have in the day. Identify how you maximise your day to dedicate time and focus on your goals.

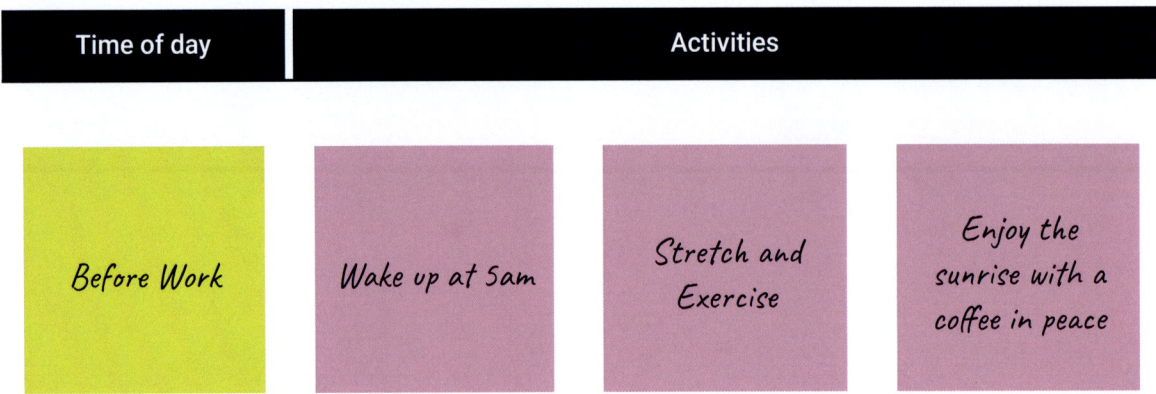

 Try sticky notes on a wall or a spreadsheet

Time of day	Activities
Morning (6am - 12pm)	Prioritise goals and objectives for the day, followed by focused time for productivity
Lunch	Exercise in the local park or quick workout on the floor at home and then have something light for lunch
Afternoon (12pm - 5pm)	Focused time for productivity
Evening (5pm - 8pm)	Decompress and take a break
Dinner	Something fun to eat
Night (8pm - 6am)	Instead of watching television; research, learn or practice new skill

PHASE FOUR: ON THE WAY

EXPERIMENT

ACTIVITY 4.1

What actions can you take to help you get from where you are to where you would like to be?

It might take one thing to achieve a goal.

It might take multiple or a combination of things to achieve a goal

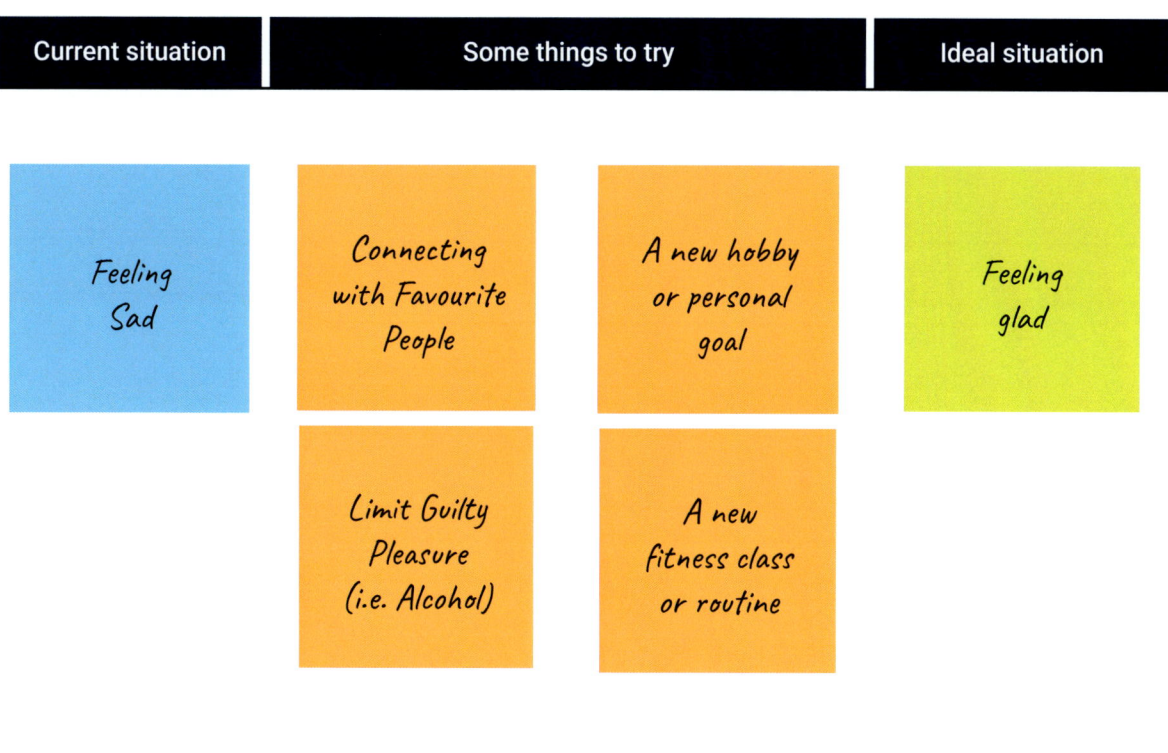

Try sticky notes on a wall

PHASE FOUR: ON THE WAY

EXPERIMENT

ACTIVITY 4.1

What actions can you take to help you get from where you are to where you would like to be?

It might take one thing to achieve a goal.

Current situation	Something to try	Ideal situation
Lose weight	Healthy Snacks	Ideal weight

It might take multiple or a combination of things to achieve a goal

Current situation	Some things to try	Ideal situation
Lose weight	Healthy snacks	Ideal weight
	Intermittent fasting	
	Walk 30 minutes every day	

EXPERIMENT

PHASE FIVE: DISRUPTIONS

PHASE FIVE:
DISRUPTIONS
———

Disruptions are a common occurrence and often out of your control. Allow time for pathways to open or consider alternative ways to make progress.

A delay whilst travelling (making progress) means the journey is ongoing and will take longer than anticipated, not that it is cancelled or impossible.

- Welcome opportunities to align with others who have shared goals
- Have patience and persistence when things don't work out as intended or adapt well to change.
- Try to maintain a healthy balance between influences or habits that give you a boost versus those that slow you down.
- When you experience delays, enjoy the moment and find a constructive way to appreciate the time.

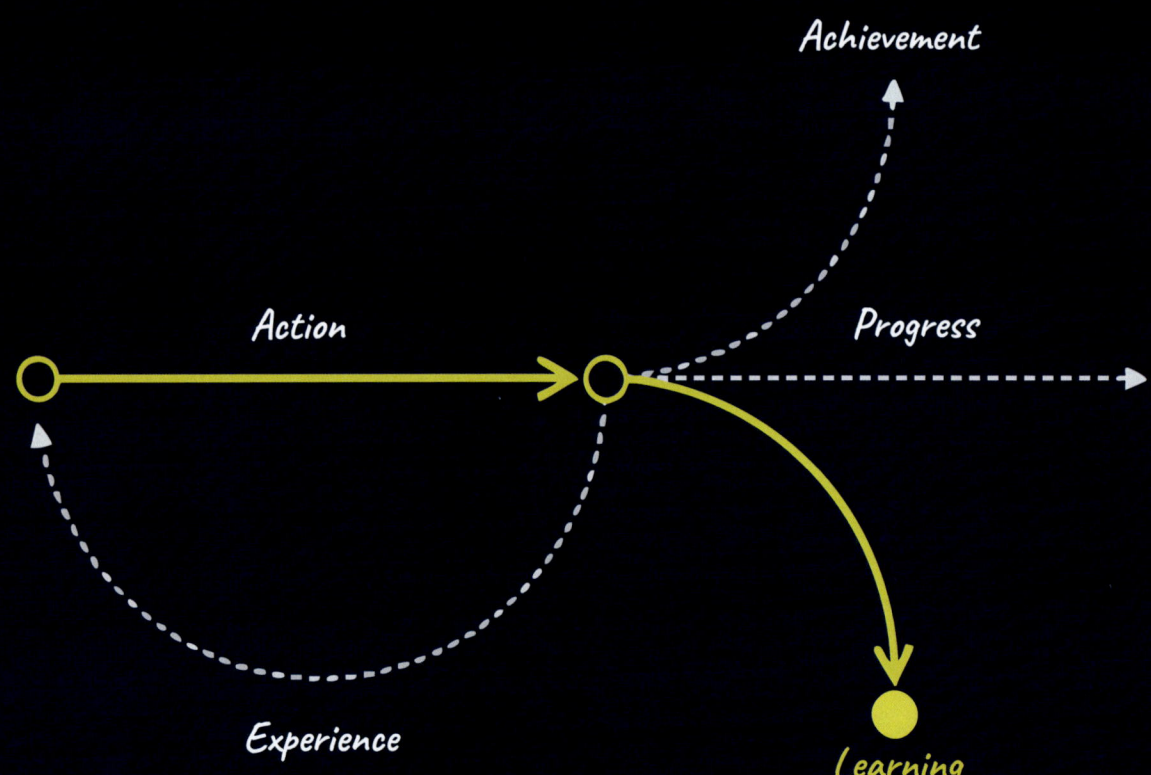

PHASE FIVE: DISRUPTIONS

Questions to help frame problems and gain perspective.
___

PHASE FIVE: DISRUPTIONS

TRAJECTORY

Avoid the pull of black holes by staying positive, maintaining momentum and remaining focused on your own path.

What might help?
 a. Gravitate towards influences that warm you up or cool you down?
 b. Focus on what's within your own atmosphere and maintaining the ecosystems for those you support?
 c. Continue along your path and avoid colliding with the paths of others?
 d. Allow yourself to become consumed by the actions and behaviours of others?

PHASE FIVE: DISRUPTIONS

MISSING PIECE

When unexpected occurrences prevent expected outcomes.
    a. Look for the missing piece?
    b. Get creative and make a new piece?
    c. Be resourceful and find an alternative piece?
    d. Accept the missing piece and appreciate the activity and unexpected outcome?
    e. Start again with a new puzzle?
    f. Give up in dissatisfaction?

PHASE FIVE: DISRUPTIONS

BLOCKED

No matter how many avenues are explored, growth can include periods of no apparent progress.

What might help?
    a. Be patient and allow time for the situation to change or conditions to improve?
    b. Embrace the opportunity to refine and exercise your approach (e.g. five unsuccessful job interviews are five chances to practice)?
    c. Refrain from being diverted, consider how to confront obstacles, create space and clear a path towards your goals?
    d. Stop, give up and assume that you've peaked and this is as far as you can go?

PHASE FIVE: DISRUPTIONS

NO WAY OUT

When it appears that there's no way out of the current situation.

What might help?
    a. Jump, discover how high you can reach when you put your mind to it?
    b. Adapt, learn new skills to help climb out of the current situation?
    c. Call for help?
    d. Wait for help?
    e. Give up and do nothing?

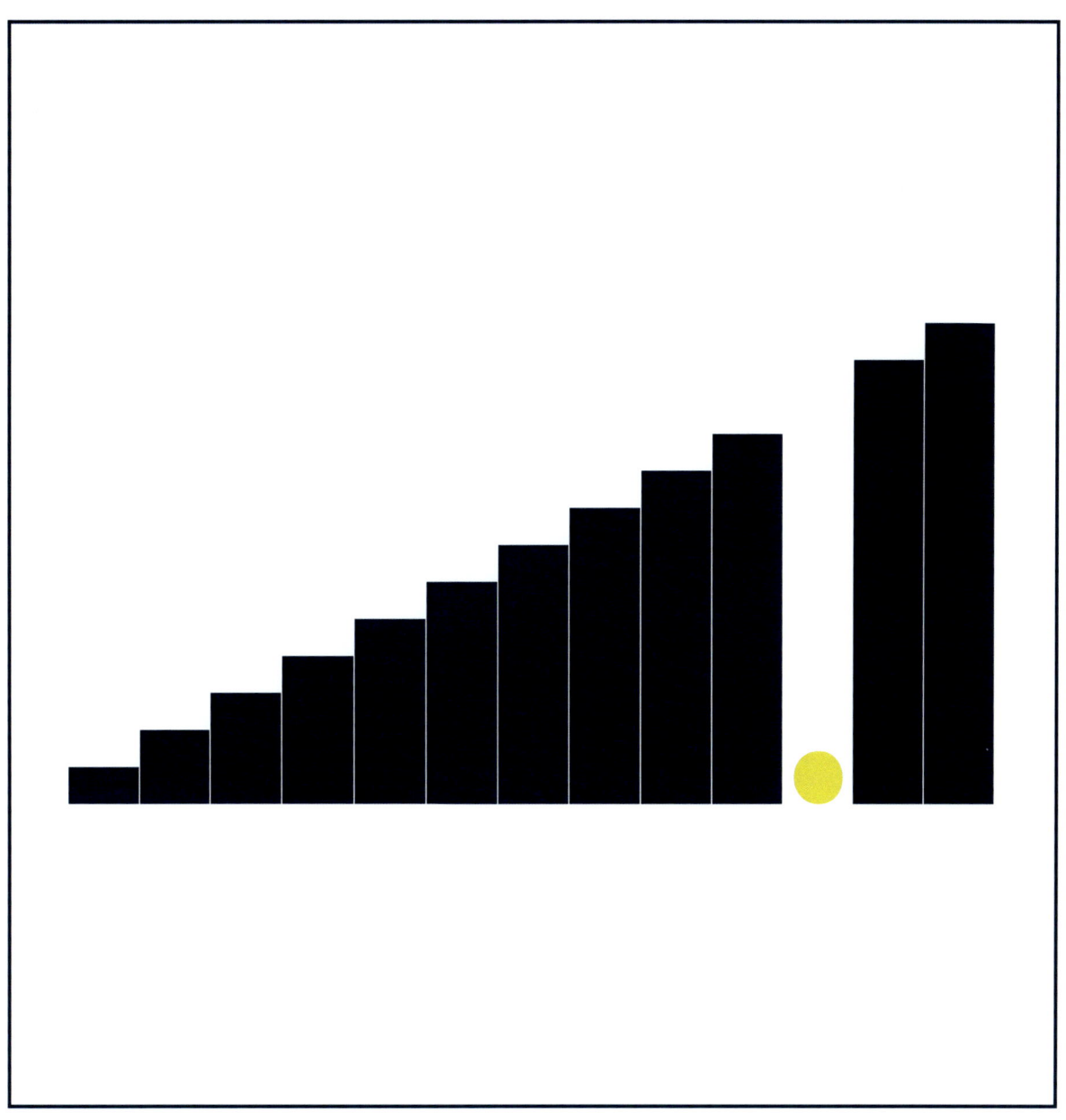

PHASE FIVE: DISRUPTIONS

OPPORTUNITIES

When the current situation, routine or interactions are less fertile, consider a change of scenery or expanding into new areas that might be more fruitful.

What might help?
  a. Talk to someone different for a change in perspective?
  b. Seek inspiration in a change of scenery?
  c. Try something new, and be open to surprises?
  d. Go beyond your comfort zone, and broaden your horizons with things that challenge you?
  e. Continue to do the same thing and expect a different outcome?

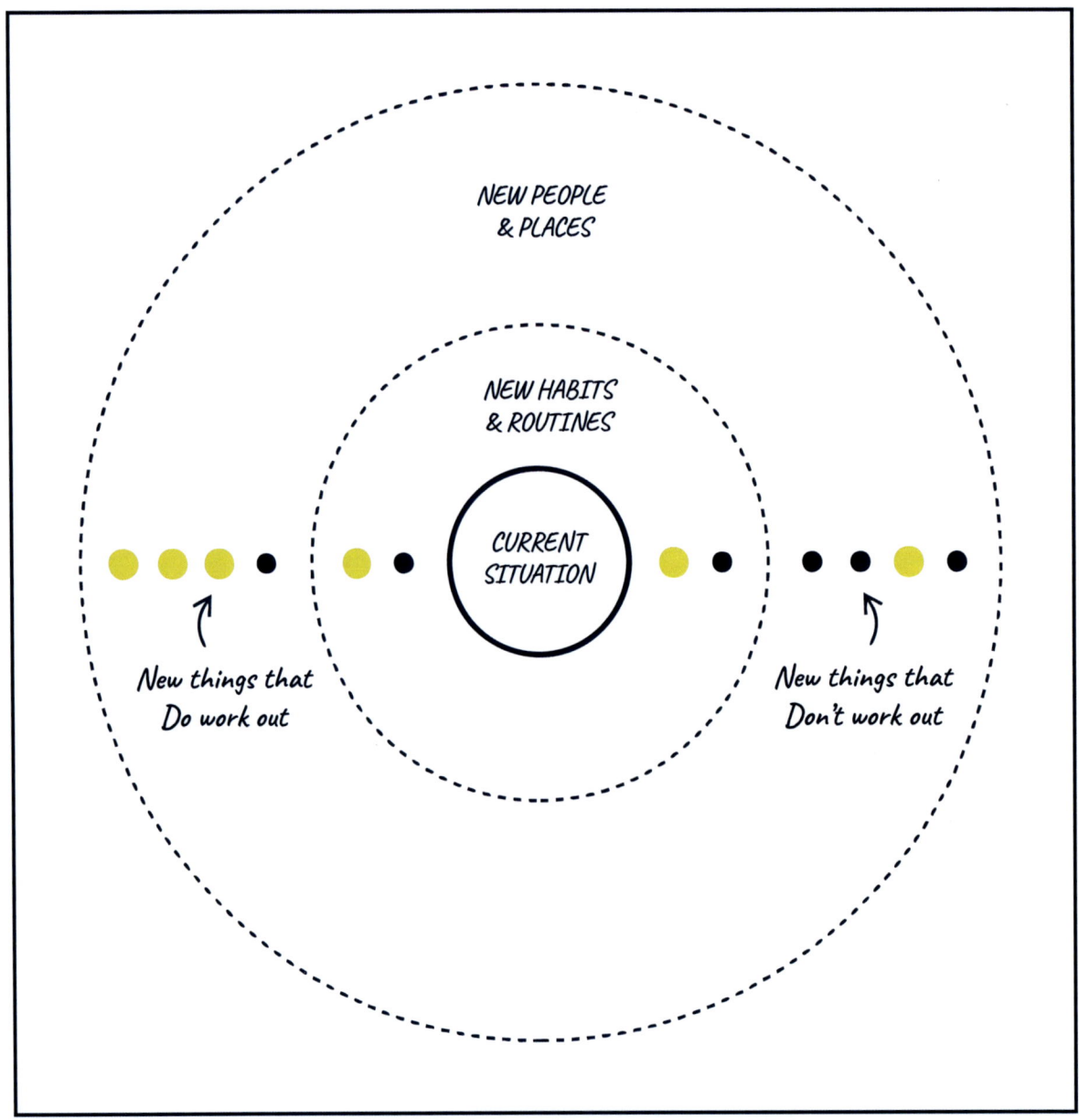

PHASE FIVE: DISRUPTIONS

ADJUSTMENTS

Focus on what is within your control to change and the actions available in the present moment.

What might help?

a. Make changes to your current routines or habits for more positive outcomes?
b. Adjust the angle of how you approach or perceive a problem or opportunity?
c. Make changes to how you use your time each day?
d. Do more of what works or feels good and less of what doesn't?
e. Focus on what is within your control to change, like what you do with your body?
f. Adjust who you spend your time with and can connect with in the present moment?
g. Attempt to adjust the past, future or actions of others?

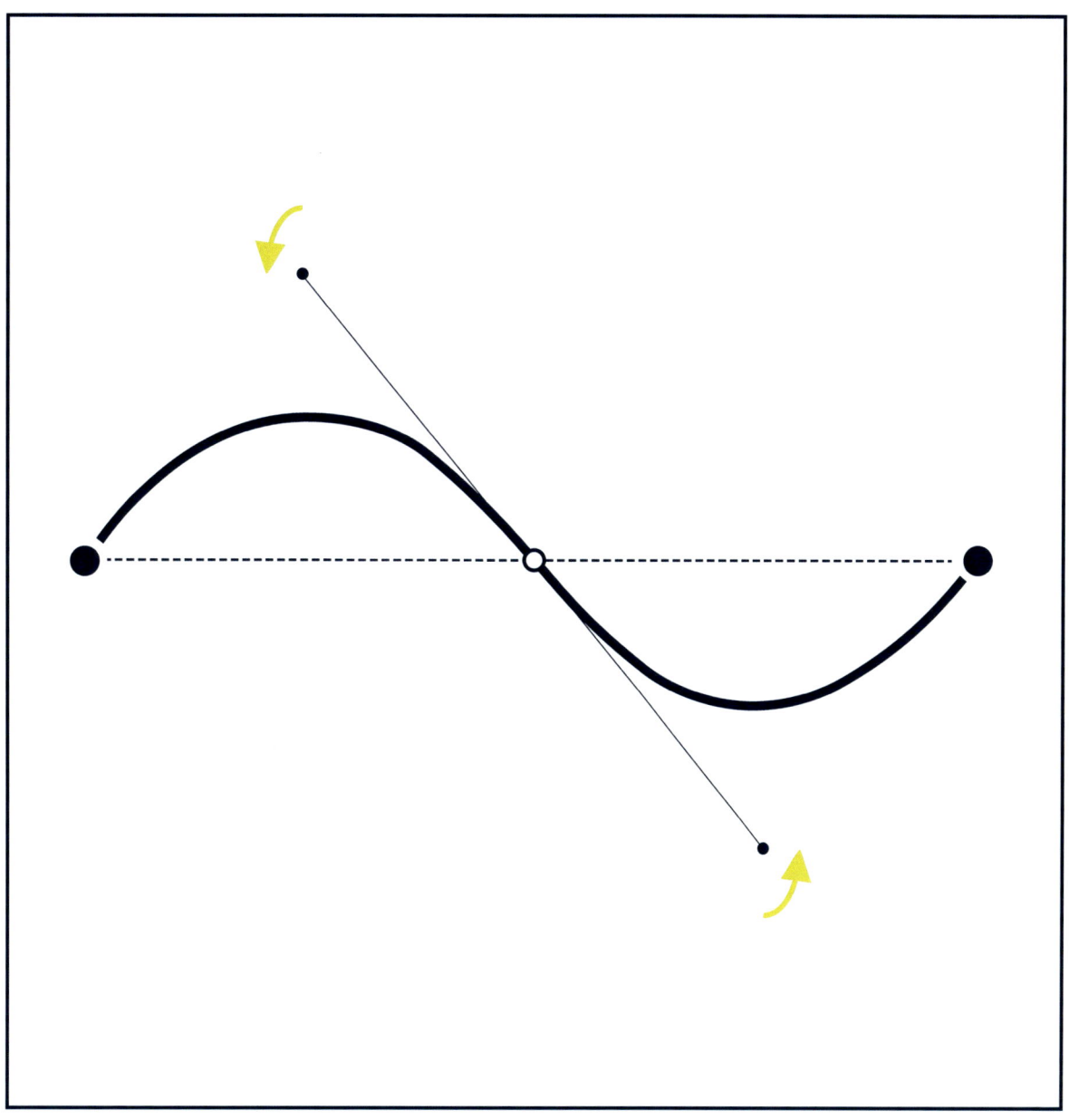

PHASE FIVE: DISRUPTIONS

OUTLOOK

Appreciating what you have and counting your blessings can help elevate when feeling low.

What might help?
    a. List three things that have gone well lately?
    b. List three things you are thankful for?
    c. List three things you enjoy doing?
    d. List three people you enjoy spending time with?
    e. Focus on what you don't have and what isn't going well?

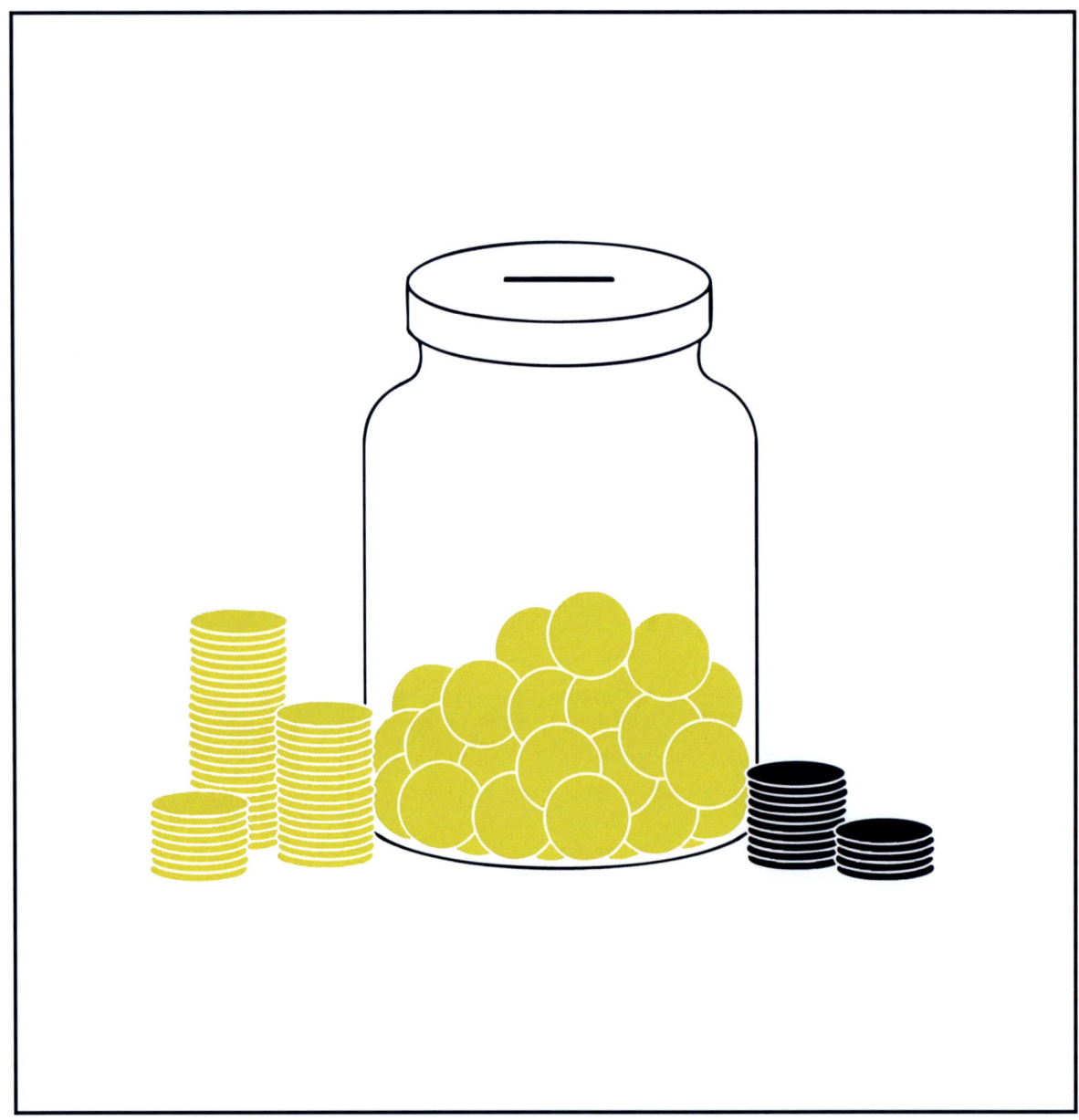

PHASE FIVE: DISRUPTIONS

REGENERATE

Making time to recharge, refresh, reflect & refocus.

What might help?
   a. Find space to refocus on something new or different for a while?
   b. Stand back to gain a fresh perspective?
   c. Take a break, take a day off or a holiday to unwind and relax?
   d. Give yourself permission to put worries aside and focus on something else?
   e. Reflect by journaling or connecting with people?
   f. Recharge by connecting with nature, meditation, stretching?
   g. Don't rest and increase the chances of stress and fatigue clouding your judgment and impacting your relationships and output?

PHASE FIVE: DISRUPTIONS

Activities to help overcome obstacles.

Negative

~~It **doesn't** often happen.~~

Positive

It **can** happen sometimes.

PHASE FIVE: DISRUPTIONS

EXPLORE

ACTIVITY 5.1

Reflect on your motivations, abilities and the support you have. Consider how you might reduce obstacles and further leverage things that help to achieve the goal you are working towards.

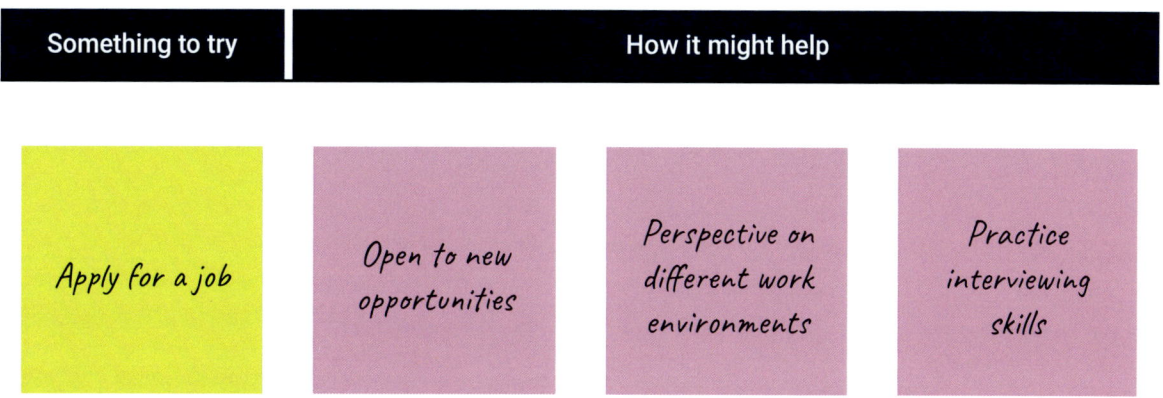

Try sticky notes on a wall or a spreadsheet

Something to try	How it might help
Coffee with someone used to work with	Expand perspective and gain career advice
Join a class	Connect with people who share similar interests
Learn a language	Stimulate the mind, impress relatives, or make travel more enjoyable.
Mentoring	Pass on my experience to help others
Volunteering with phone services that support older people and those in distress	Use my empathy skills to help others
Reduce alcohol/junk food intake	Increase likeliness to work on goals or exercise that day or the following day

PHASE FIVE: DISRUPTIONS

REFINE

ACTIVITY 5.2

Reflect on your motivations, abilities and the support you have. Consider how you might reduce obstacles and further leverage things that help to achieve the goal you are working towards.

Try sticky notes on a wall

66

PHASE FIVE: DISRUPTIONS

BALANCE

ACTIVITY 5.3

Reflect on your habits and routines. Can you make any changes or improvements to increase your chances of success?

How might you prioritise how you spend your time? When are you most productive?

Try *sticky notes* on a wall or a *spreadsheet*

I should keep doing	I should stop doing	I should start doing
Drinking plenty of water	Working through lunch	Create more time by waking up at 5:00 am

BALANCE

PHASE FIVE: DISRUPTIONS

TRANSITIONING FROM HOLIDAY TO WORK

ACTIVITY 5.4

Returning to work after some time off can be daunting, especially if there are specific reasons for not wanting to return. Having a balanced view can help with the transition back to work.

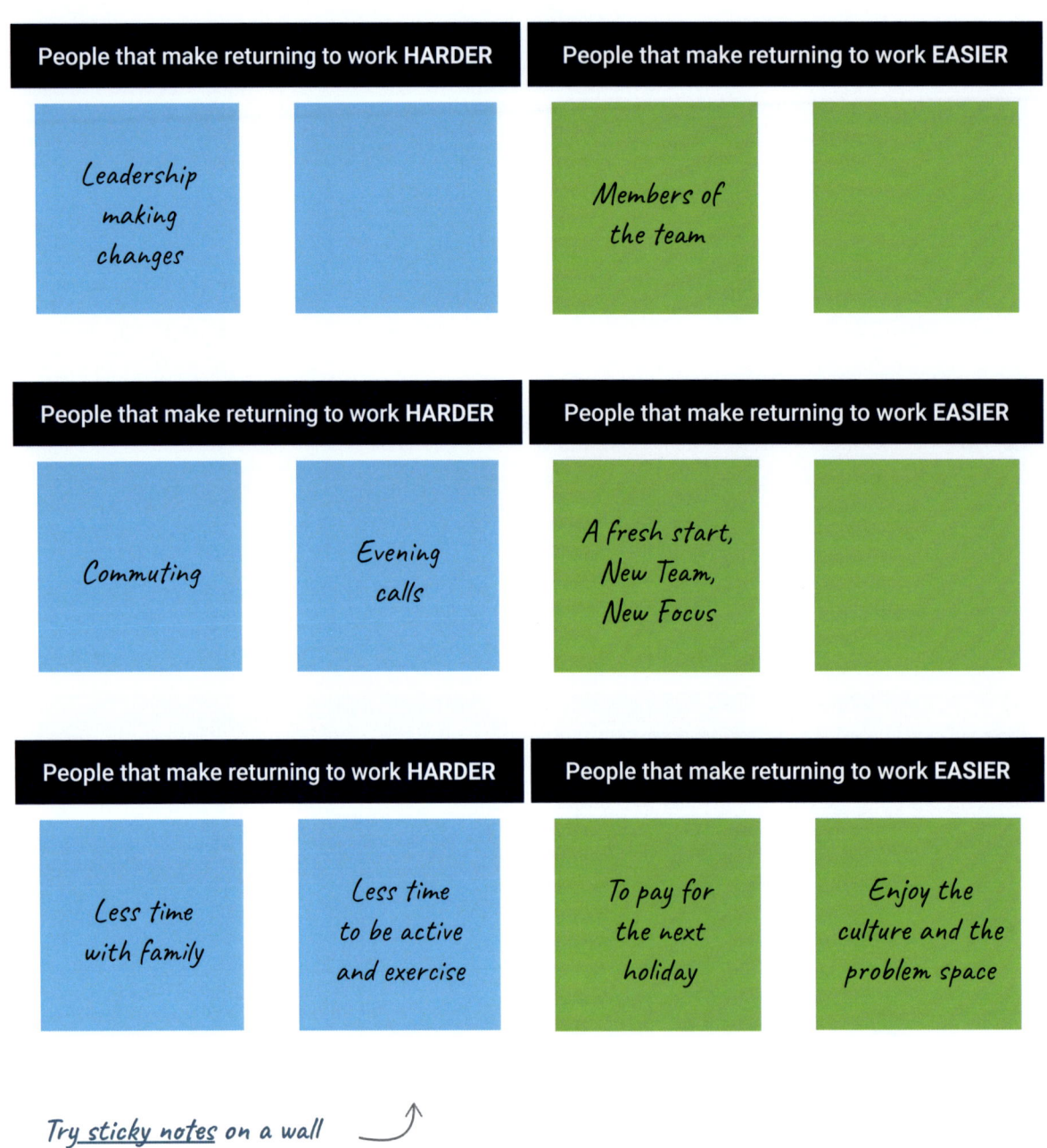

People that make returning to work HARDER	People that make returning to work EASIER
Leadership making changes	Members of the team
Commuting / Evening calls	A fresh start, New Team, New Focus
Less time with family / Less time to be active and exercise	To pay for the next holiday / Enjoy the culture and the problem space

Try sticky notes on a wall →

68

PHASE SIX: CANCELLATIONS

When travelling or making progress from one situation or place to another is cancelled, not all travel or progress is cancelled. Only that particular situation at that moment in time is cancelled. There will be other opportunities to make progress and alternative ways to achieve similar outcomes.

From birth, we learn that learning to walk does not come without some falls and that failure is often part of the process towards making improvements.

For example, a cancelled holiday doesn't mean you'll never go on holiday again. There's an opportunity to reflect on where you want to go, decide on the most pleasant way to get there and what you have to look forward to when you arrive. The same might apply to a failed job interview or a bad dating experience.

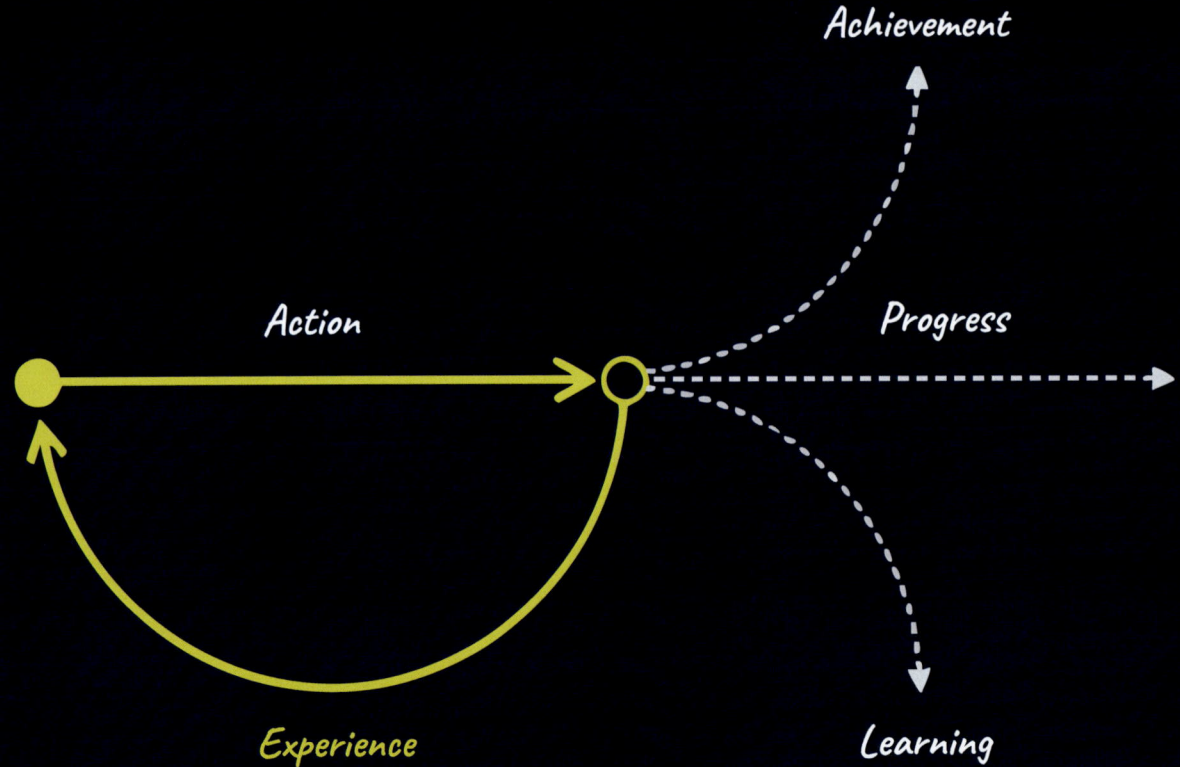

PHASE SIX: CANCELLATIONS

Questions to help frame problems and gain perspective.
———

PHASE SIX: CANCELLATIONS

DISORIENTATED

Making progress when it feels like going around in circles and not accomplishing very much.

What might help?
    a. Have patience. Sometimes things take longer than expected to complete?
    b. Keep going and continue to make progress towards your goal?
    c. Break the feeling of repetition by speeding up or slowing down to make more rapid or considerate progress?
    d. Continue to practice, refine and narrow down your approach towards your goal?
    e. Stop before you complete the process because taking longer than expected?

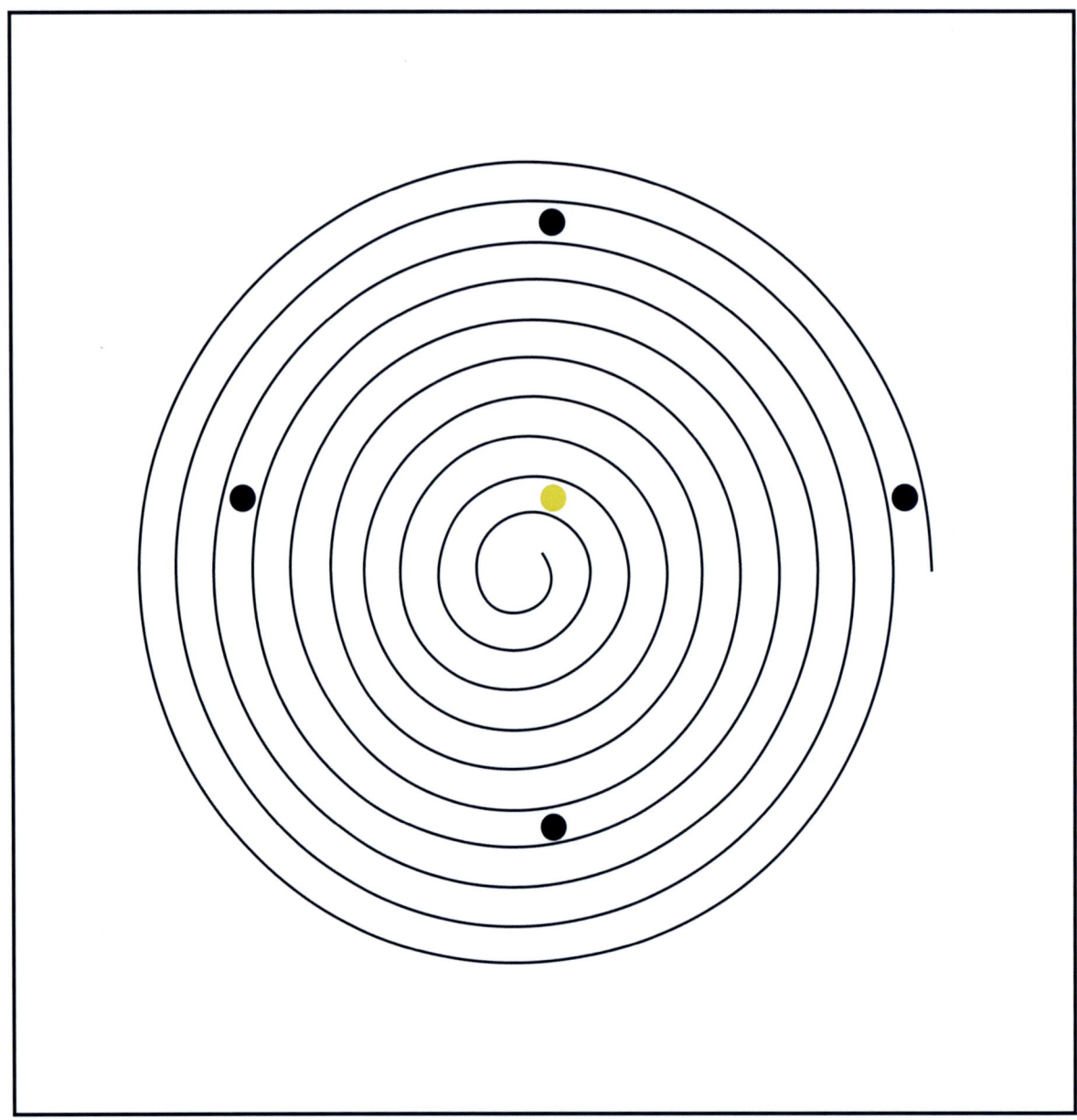

PHASE SIX: CANCELLATIONS

A NEW DAY

When yesterday didn't work out as expected, the unexpected can surprise you today and tomorrow.

What might help?
  a. Reflect on your goals and decide whether to try again or pivot to something else?
  b. Reevaluate your approach and alternative ways to make progress?
  c. Consider viewing a missed opportunity as a blessing in disguise?
  d. Win the day before it starts by waking up early to do something productive?
  e. Plenty of fish are in the sea, and today might surprise you?
  f. Be open and receptive to new experiences, encounters and opportunities?
  g. Dwell on what could have been and live in the past?

PHASE SIX: CANCELLATIONS

TESTING

Knowing if you'll enjoy or be good at something is easier if you've given it a go.

What might help?
   a. Try again. You have what it takes to succeed and were unlucky on this particular occasion?
   b. Continue to explore your options until something works out?
   c. Make your own options and opportunities?
   d. Don't take risks, shy away from new experiences and stick with what you know?

PHASE SIX: CANCELLATIONS

PATIENCE

When it feels like waiting in line as others appear to skip and make quicker progress.

What might help?
   a. Avoid comparing yourself to others; they may have been lucky, working harder or waiting longer than you realise?
   b. Make the most of the extra time you have to prepare, anticipate or plan?
   c. Try to rush the process before you're ready or when the timing is right?
   d. Stop trying and give up because progress is taking too long?

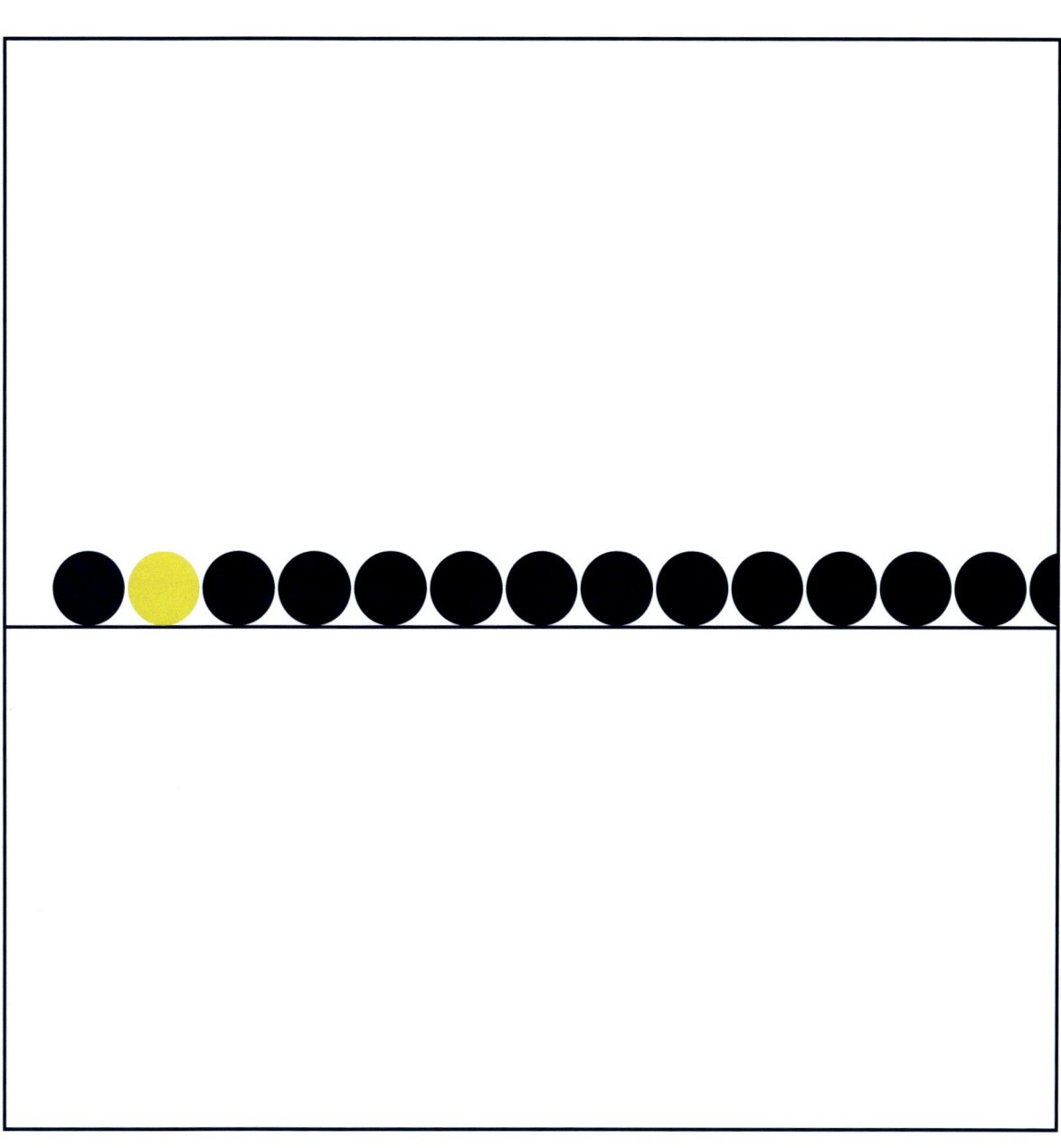

PHASE SIX: CANCELLATIONS

PERSEVERANCE

Working harder to keep up or achieve similar results.

What might help?
    a. Consider gaining new skills or abilities that will increase your chances of success?
    b. Appreciate that you might be progressing in other aspects of your life that others might be struggling with?
    c. Recognise and focus on your strengths to make more effective progress?
    d. Embrace the opportunity to practice and improve?
    e. Value your dedication and strong work ethic to drive change and make progress.
    f. Give up when things get hard and fall further behind?

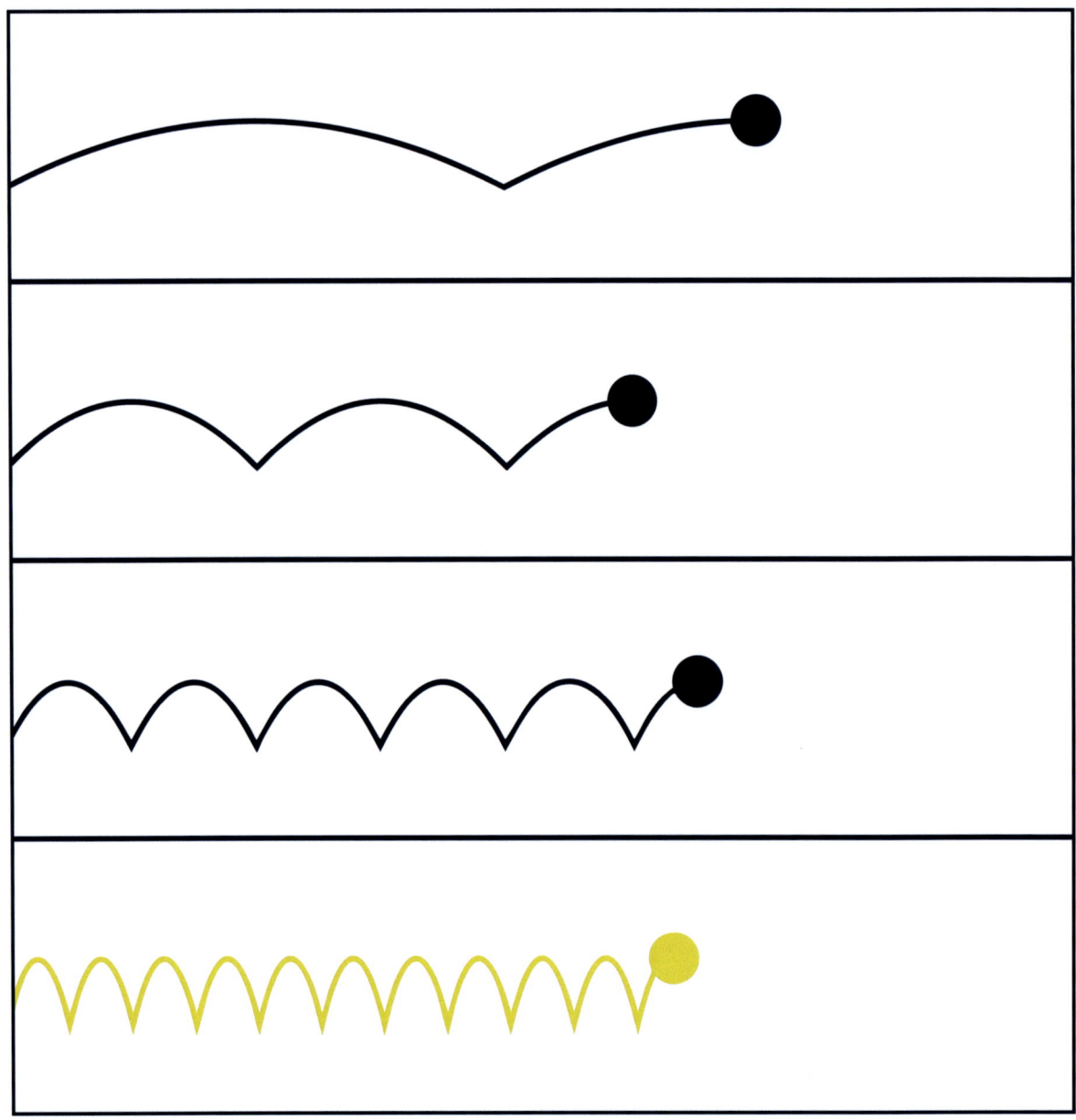

PHASE SIX: CANCELLATIONS

STIMULANTS

Growth can occur when nurtured under the right conditions.

What might help?
- a. Make time for those you like to spend time with?
- b. Make time for the activities you enjoy?
- c. Make time to regain strength with diet and exercise?
- d. Make time to recover with rest, relaxation and entertainment?
- e. Make time to feed your mind with something informative or inspiring?
- f. Make time to connect with nature for a change of scenery and perspective?
- g. Power through, refraining from making time for perceived distractions (rest and exercise) in favour of real distractions and the ability to be effective (fatigue)?

PHASE SIX: CANCELLATIONS

Activities to help evolve and adapt to setbacks.

Negative

Expecting **different** *results by doing the same thing over and over again.*

Positive

Expecting **better** *results by doing the same thing over and over again.*

PHASE SIX: CANCELLATIONS

RECOVERY

ACTIVITY 6.1

Consider if there is anything you can introduce to routine to maintain your health and wellbeing. Mental stimulation, eating healthy, drinking water, getting enough sleep and exercising can be good places to start when taking care of yourself.

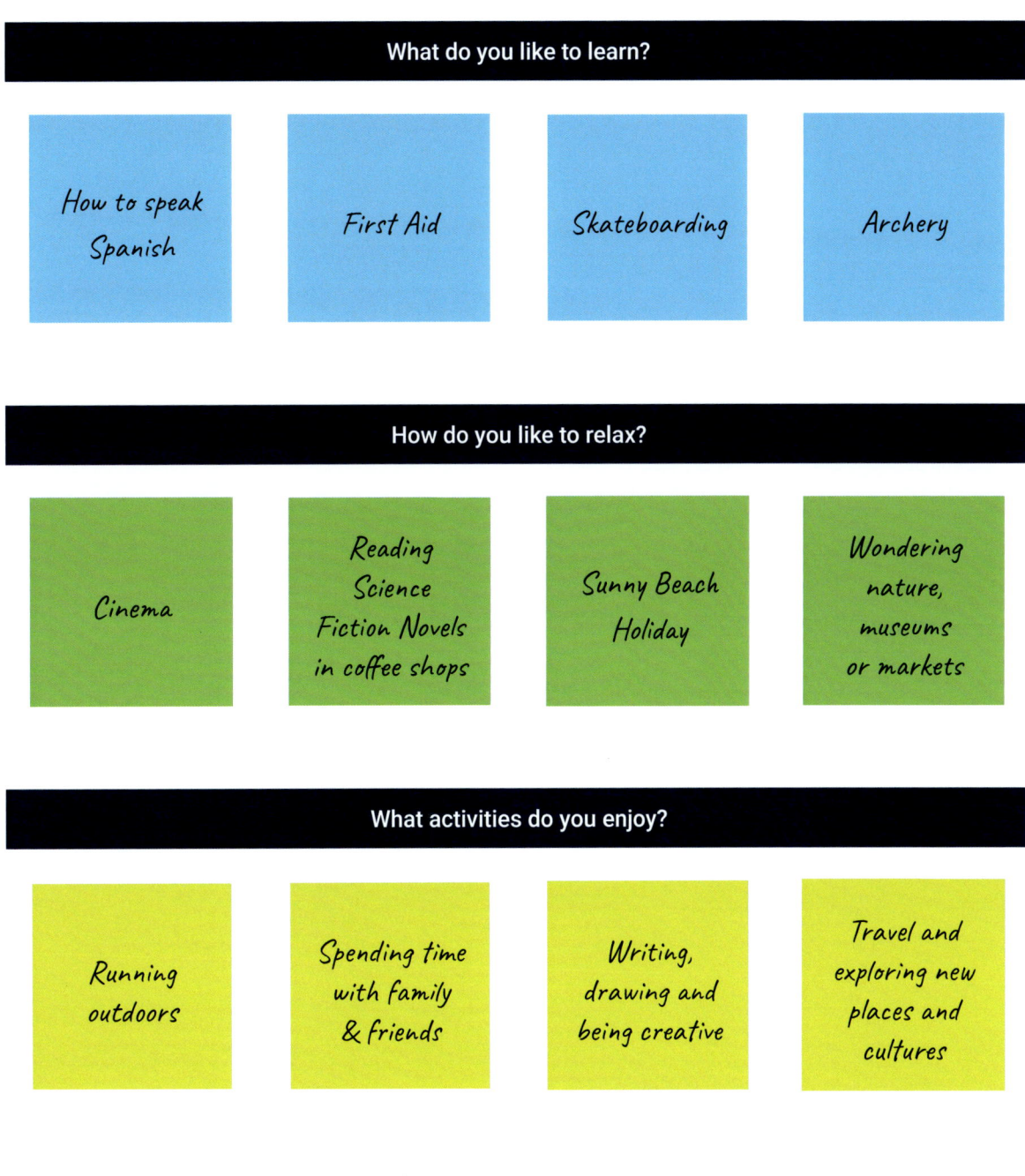

What do you like to learn?

| How to speak Spanish | First Aid | Skateboarding | Archery |

How do you like to relax?

| Cinema | Reading Science Fiction Novels in coffee shops | Sunny Beach Holiday | Wondering nature, museums or markets |

What activities do you enjoy?

| Running outdoors | Spending time with family & friends | Writing, drawing and being creative | Travel and exploring new places and cultures |

Try sticky notes on a wall

PHASE SIX: CANCELLATIONS

CALIBRATION

ACTIVITY 6.2

Strike a balance between relaxation, procrastination and productivity by reflecting on how much time/energy you spend on distractions versus how much time/energy you dedicate working towards an ideal situation.

Try _sticky notes_ on a wall or a _spreadsheet_

Distractions	Working towards new situation
Streaming entertainment	Studying
Unhealthy snacks	Creating distance from the fridge at home by going to the gym
Limit Guilty Pleasure (i.e. Alcohol)	Learning a new skill

PHASE SIX: CANCELLATIONS

EFFICIENCIES

ACTIVITY 6.3

Reflect on how you spend your spare time. Identify any distractions or unproductive behaviours. Then think about stimulating or constructive behaviours that encourage growth, good health and wellbeing; consider how to find a balance to maximise your time.

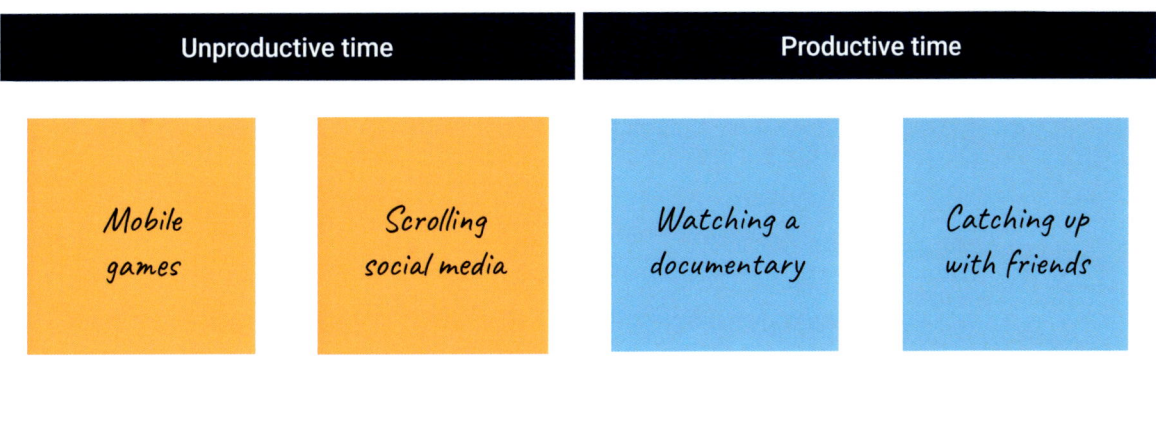

Try *sticky notes* on a wall or a *spreadsheet*

Unproductive time	Productive time
Time spent on the couch	*Time spent in nature, exercising, learning something new or getting more sleep.*

81

PHASE SEVEN: ARRIVAL

PHASE SEVEN:

ARRIVAL

Congratulations, you've navigated time and space to progress towards a goal, new environment or situation.

- Take a moment to celebrate your accomplishment and relish the experience and excitement before you become acclimatised?
- Recognise and appreciate who and what helped you arrive at your goal?
- Take a break and recharge your batteries before you get busy again?
- Take a deep breath and explore your new situation and all the new possibilities that have been unlocked?
- Look around and acknowledge what may have changed, what has remained, what have you let go of, and what have you picked up that's new?

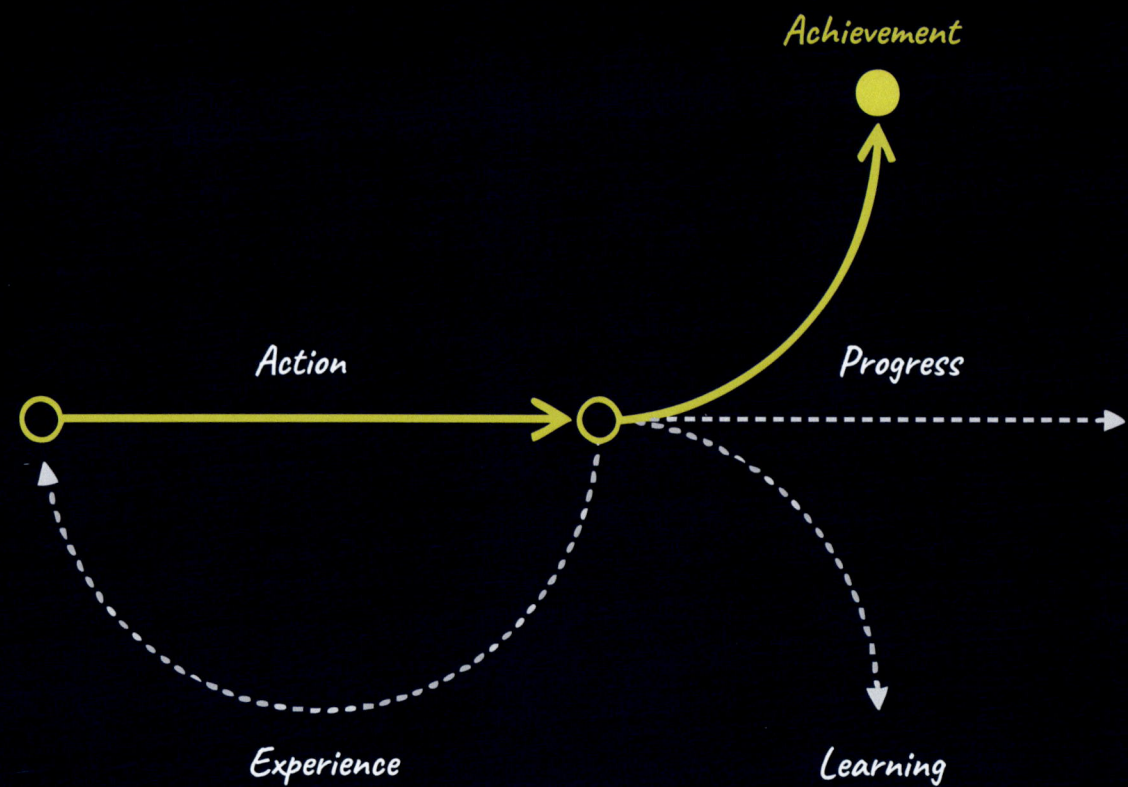

PHASE SEVEN: ARRIVAL

Questions to help frame problems and gain perspective.
___

PHASE SEVEN: ARRIVAL

PERSISTENCE

It only takes one positive response; anything else is just practice.

When results aren't instant, it can fuel the perception that time and effort have been wasted. On the contrary, feedback and practice were part of the process and essential to your success.

For example, several failed job interviews provided opportunities for free advice from experts in the field to practice your story and explore what resonates and what needs refining.

PHASE SEVEN: ARRIVAL

APPRECIATION

Making progress from one situation to another is a social activity that involves the presence, support, guidance and benefit of others.

Even when you felt alone, others lived alongside and around you. Recognise the moments of support or alignment you shared. Appreciate the relationships and connections with those you encountered on the way that provided fleeting or recurring meaningful moments of comfort and inspiration.

Embrace opportunities to be there for others needing support on their journey.

PHASE SEVEN: ARRIVAL

SERENDIPITY

Things didn't go to plan or work out as expected, but that's okay.

The most direct path isn't always the most enjoyable or inspiring way to get from one situation to another.

When a journey takes longer than expected, you've likely gained more experiences, memories and learnings than expected. Sometimes, things don't work out as planned because there are unanticipated obstacles to navigate or unexpected opportunities to embrace.

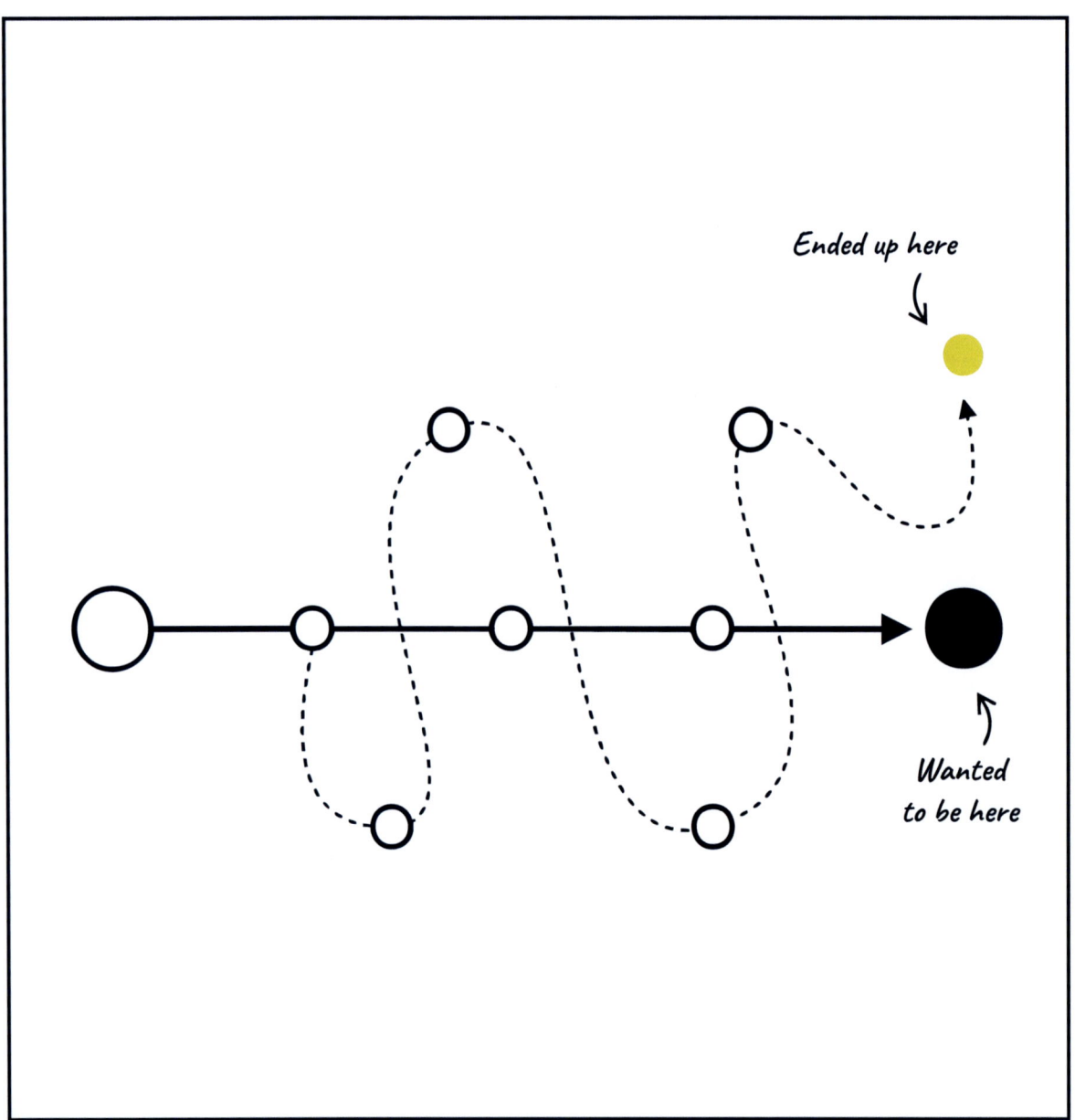

PHASE SEVEN: ARRIVAL

TRANSITION

Celebrate accomplishments, acknowledge hard work and take a break.

Take time out to detach from one situation before you move to another with some rest and recreation. Your new environment will likely provide plenty of new connections, information and opportunities to process and different routines and requirements to accommodate.

PHASE SEVEN: ARRIVAL

Activities to help find value in the journey.

―――

Negative

~~A journey might take longer than expected.~~

Positive

A journey might provide more experience than expected.

PHASE SEVEN: ARRIVAL

REFLECT

ACTIVITY 7.1

Recognise and appreciate who and what helped you arrive at your goal. Consider if the ingredients for success are unique to this particular accomplishment or transferrable to other goals.

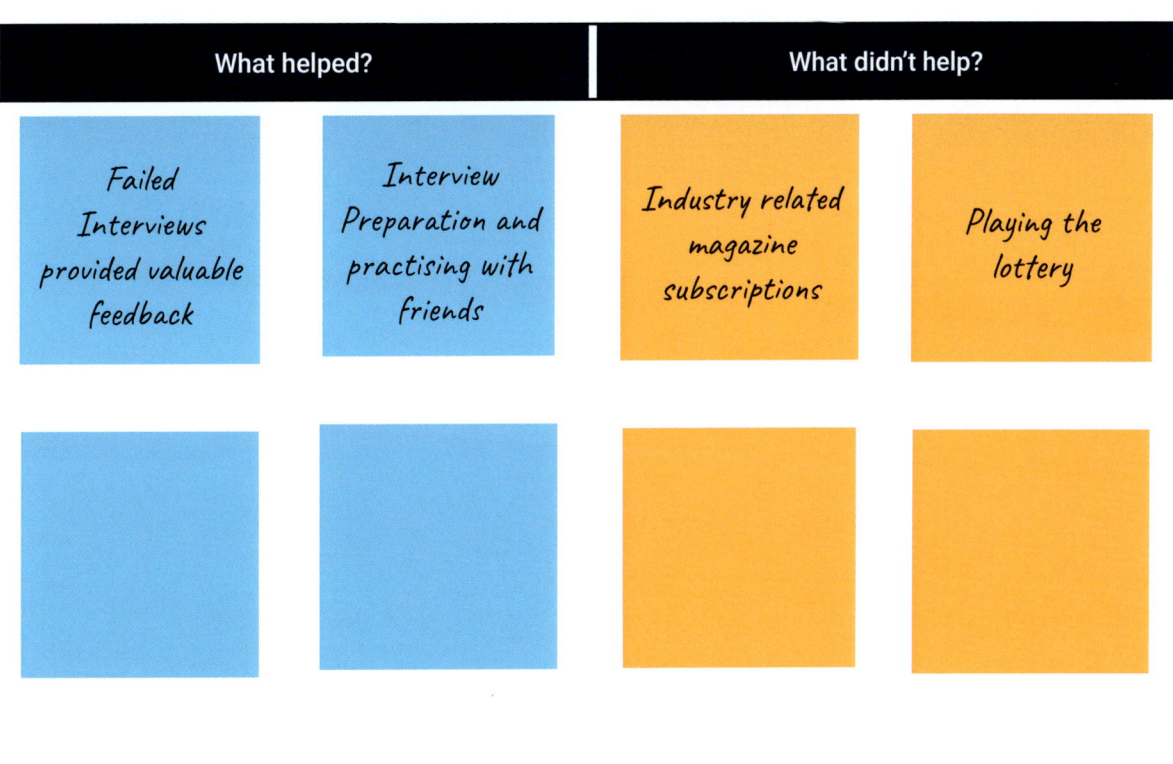

Try sticky notes on a wall.

PHASE SEVEN: ARRIVAL

MOVING ON

ACTIVITY 7.2

Look around and acknowledge what may have changed, what has remained the same. Perhaps this is an excellent time to let go or remove old habits or commitments in exchange for new ones.

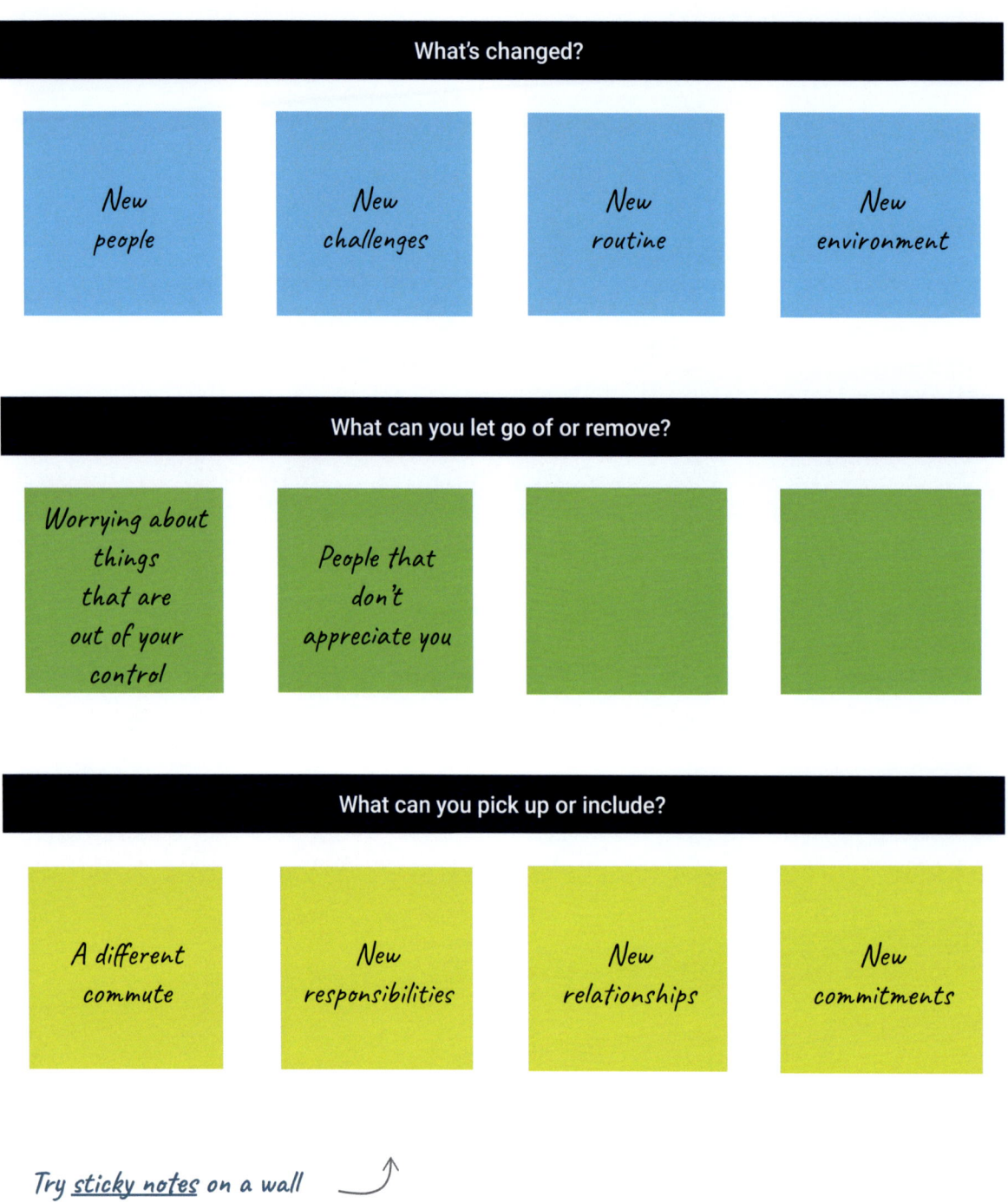

What's changed?			
New people	New challenges	New routine	New environment

What can you let go of or remove?			
Worrying about things that are out of your control	People that don't appreciate you		

What can you pick up or include?			
A different commute	New responsibilities	New relationships	New commitments

Try *sticky notes* on a wall

PHASE SEVEN: ARRIVAL

MISSION (*IMPOSSIBLE*) POSSIBLE

ACTIVITY 7.3

Congratulations, you have another item to add to the list of unexpected achievements. Reflect on what made it possible and what you did to enable the situation.

Remember that you can do great things. You've done it before, and you can do it again.

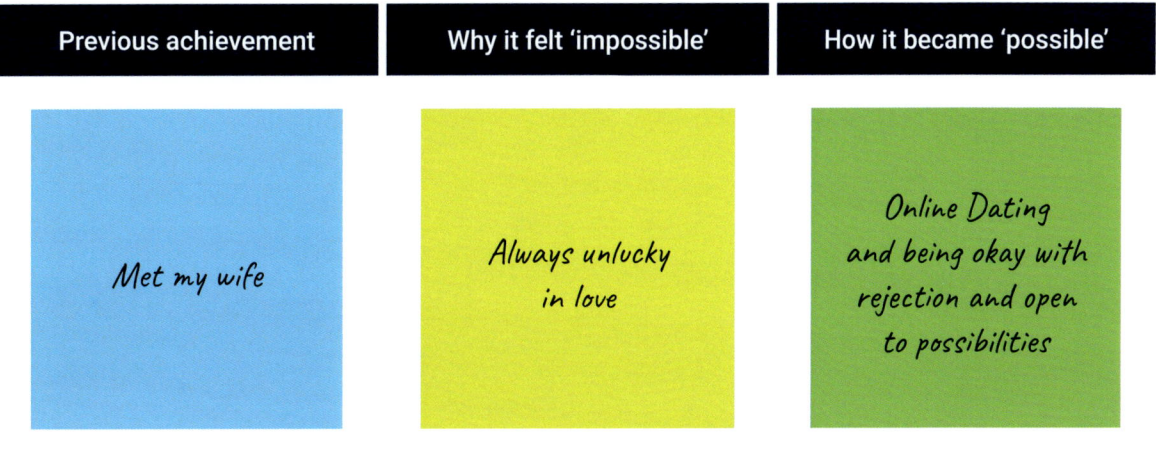

Try <u>sticky notes</u> on a wall or a <u>spreadsheet</u>

Previous achievement	Why it felt 'impossible'	How it became 'possible'
Living and working in America for a few years	No job, no visa, no money, no place to stay	The support of college friends and their relatives in America.

91

PHASE EIGHT: WHAT NOW

PHASE EIGHT:
WHAT NOW

―――――

You suddenly find yourself out of your comfort zone and in unfamiliar territory where relatively simple tasks can become more challenging, including where to start and how to navigate all the uncertainty and ambiguity.

Take one thing at a time and have confidence in your abilities to adapt and acclimatise to problems and opportunities because you've risen to the challenge before and can do it again.

- New connections and relationships
- New rhythms and routines
- New possibilities and inspiration
- New understanding of what works and what doesn't
- New problems and responsibilities
- New moments and experiences
- New skills and challenges

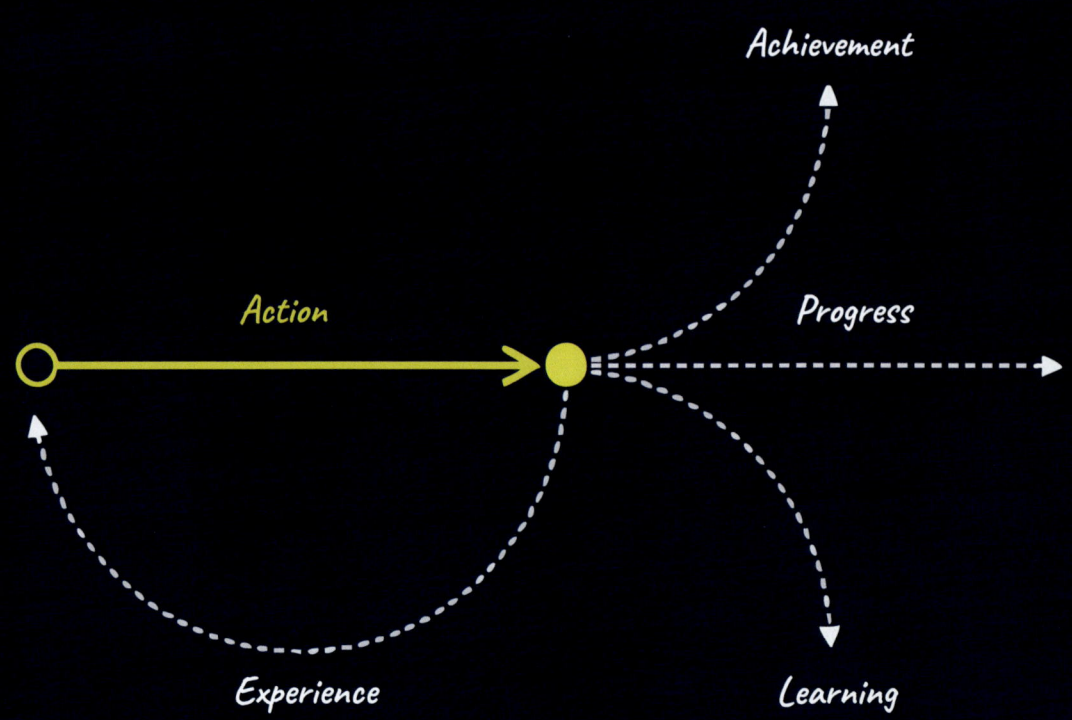

PHASE EIGHT: WHAT NOW

Activities to help evolve and adapt to setbacks.
———

PHASE EIGHT: WHAT NOW

OUT OF DEPTH

Feeling out of depth in new and unfamiliar environments when there is much to establish, rebuild and understand.

What might help?
- a. Project confidence that you won't sink by casually probing others for advice without exposing your insecurities?
- b. Identify a quick win that puts wind in your sails and makes a great first impression. Helping others and being helpful can be a great place to start?
- c. Seek collaboration to provide support and keep you afloat?
- d. Ease in gently and give yourself time to breathe and adapt?
- e. Overcompensate by diving in, making a splash and making a spectacle of yourself?

PHASE EIGHT: WHAT NOW

THE BIG PICTURE

When facing a new challenge, it can take time to identify what's important and understand how it all fits together.

What might help?
    a. Start with what's familiar; the rest will come later?
    b. Learn from the experience of others?
    c. Compile a list of concerns, confusions and assumptions and tick them off as your understanding grows?
    d. Have fun, and think of the problem as a puzzle to solve?
    e. Become impatient and act without being adequately informed?

PHASE EIGHT: WHAT NOW

FINDING A WAY

New situations can be challenging and confusing to navigate.

What might help?
  a. Have patience. It takes time to navigate ambiguity?
  b. Stay positive. Making mistakes is part of the process?
  c. Be comfortable. Not having all the answers is expected?
  d. Have fun. View obstacles as challenges to overcome?
  e. Panic. Assume you'll never find a way out and be lost forever?

PHASE EIGHT: WHAT NOW

PERSPECTIVE

Maintaining an open mind when encountering new situations, as appearances can be deceiving depending on your perspective or point of view.

What might help?
   a. People can surprise you, refrain from judgements based on first impressions?
   b. People can surprise you, be careful with how much you share upfront?
   c. View a problem as an opportunity that isn't correctly understood?
   d. Attempt to understand the problem from an alternative point of view?
   e. Seek a second opinion or another perspective?
   f. Sometimes a wall is a wall, and there's no way forward?

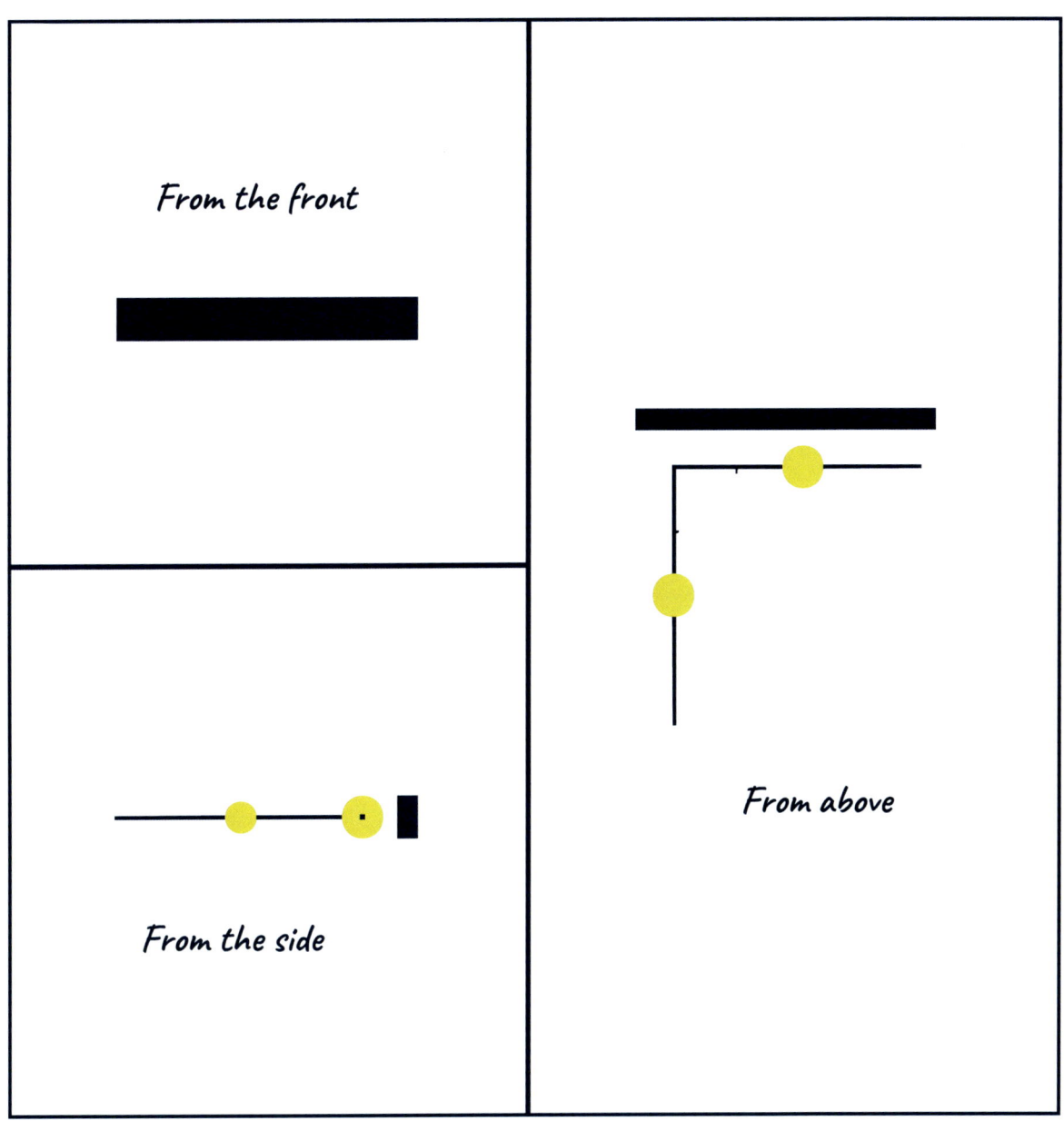

PHASE EIGHT: WHAT NOW

PERSEVERANCE

Adapting to new situations can come with highs and lows, where some days go more smoothly than others.

What might help?
   a. Stay positive and focus on what's going well?
   b. When feeling low, try focusing on being busy, productive and helpful?
   c. Have patience. The current mood is a moment in time that will pass?
   d. Seek reassurance from others that have been in your situation?
   e. Go with the flow. Highs and lows are a natural part of the process?
   f. Go easy on yourself. Everybody has good days and bad days?
   g. Continue to doubt and question yourself as it keeps you on your toes?

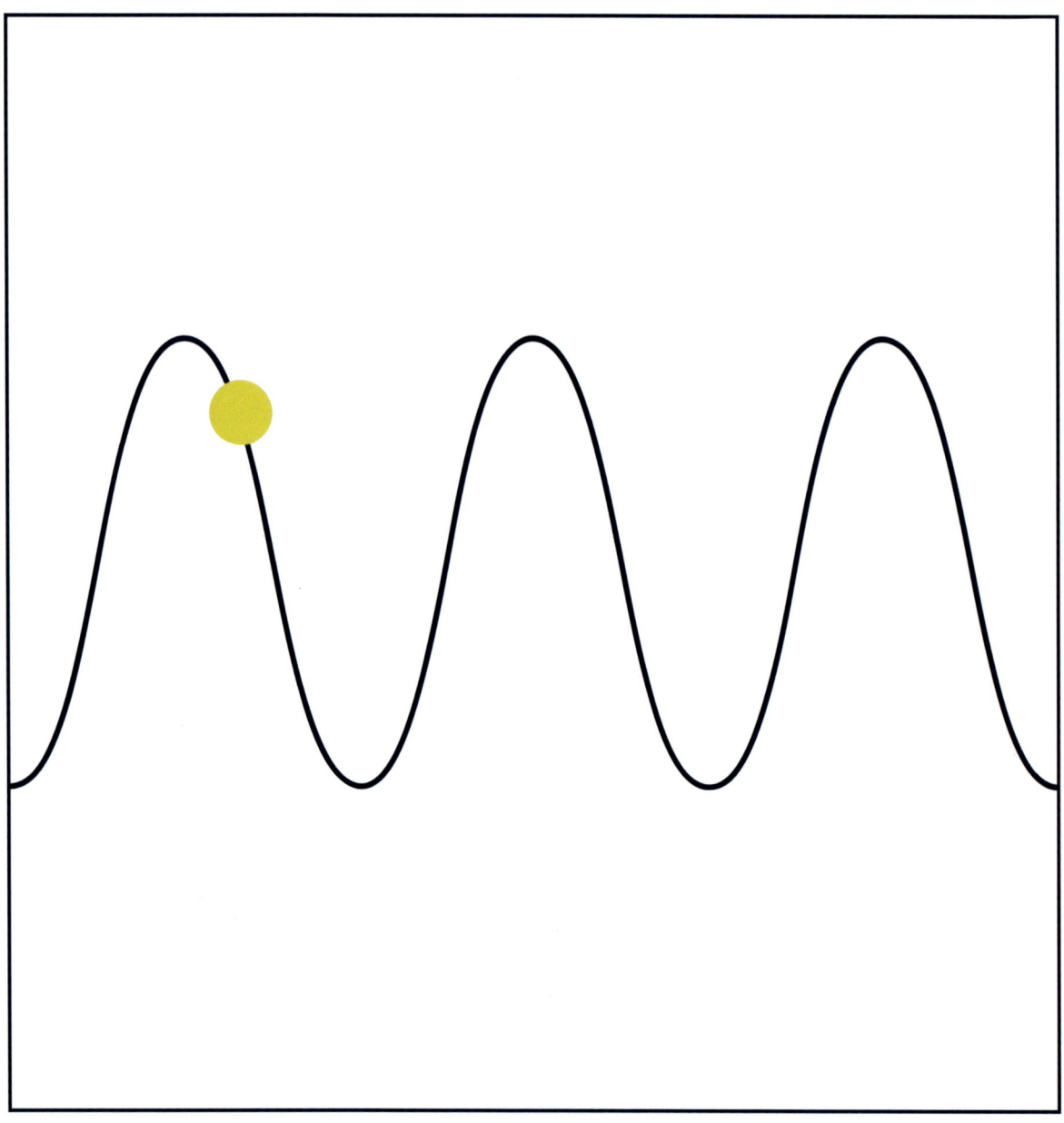

PHASE EIGHT: WHAT NOW

Activities to help acclimatise to new situations.

Negative

~~I **don't** know what I am doing.~~

Positive

I **will** know what I am doing.

PHASE EIGHT: WHAT NOW

HELPFUL HABITS

ACTIVITY 8.1

Create time for coping mechanisms that help to process and adapt to new situations. For example, start your day by making a list of things to do so you're not overwhelmed and making time each week to decompress with friends and family.

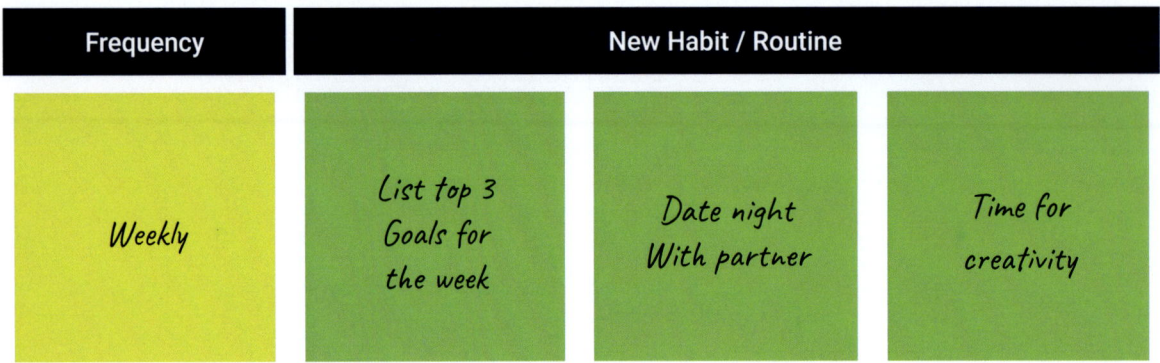

Frequency	New Habit / Routine		
Weekly	List top 3 Goals for the week	Date night With partner	Time for creativity

Try sticky notes on a wall or a spreadsheet

Time of day	Activities / Actions
Daily	Wake up at 5am to create extra time
2-3 Times a Week	Yoga
Weekly	Dedicated time to focus and work on personal goals without distractions
Weekends	Long runs along the river or road-trips with family or friends
Bi-Weekly	Connect with friends
Monthly	Participate in a class to learn a new skill and connect with people who have similar interests (e.g. painting, archery, cooking classes)
Annually	Participate in a sporting event (e.g. marathon, a charity hike or mountain climb)

PHASE EIGHT: WHAT NOW

BALANCE

ACTIVITY 8.2

Lean on the things that helped you once before and continue to leverage the habits and routines you introduced to maintain your wellbeing and increase your chances of success.

Try sticky notes on a wall or a spreadsheet

Continue doing	Stop doing	Try doing
Taking regular breaks to stretch and breathe	An unhealthy diet because it's convenient	Preparing healthy snacks in advance

PHASE NINE:
WHAT NEXT

Opportunities are everywhere and hopefully this book has helped to better identify and leverage them.

When you are ready, take the next step and keep the momentum going.
- How might you improve your current situation?
- How might you expand on your current situation?
- How might you learn from your current situation?
- How might you appreciate your current situation?
- How might you change your current situation?

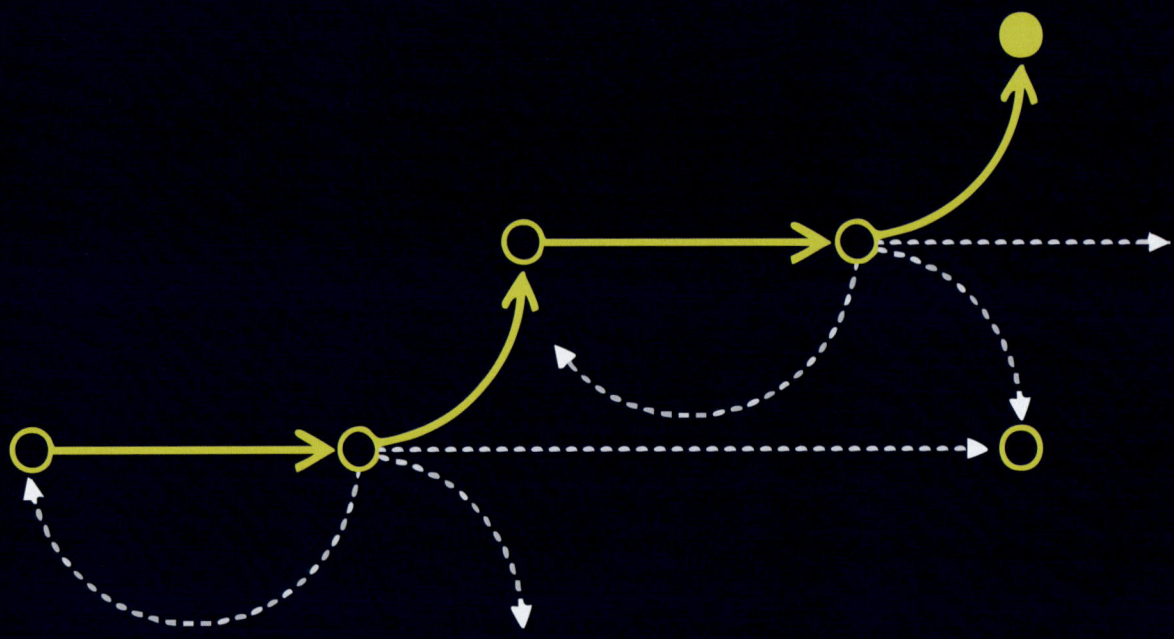

PHASE NINE: WHAT NEXT

LOOKING AHEAD

Again, Picture yourself five years from now; what would you like to see?

What might help?
    a. Everything is the same?
    b. New or improved skills?
    c. New or improved home?
    d. New or improved job?
    e. New or improved relationships?
    f. Something else?

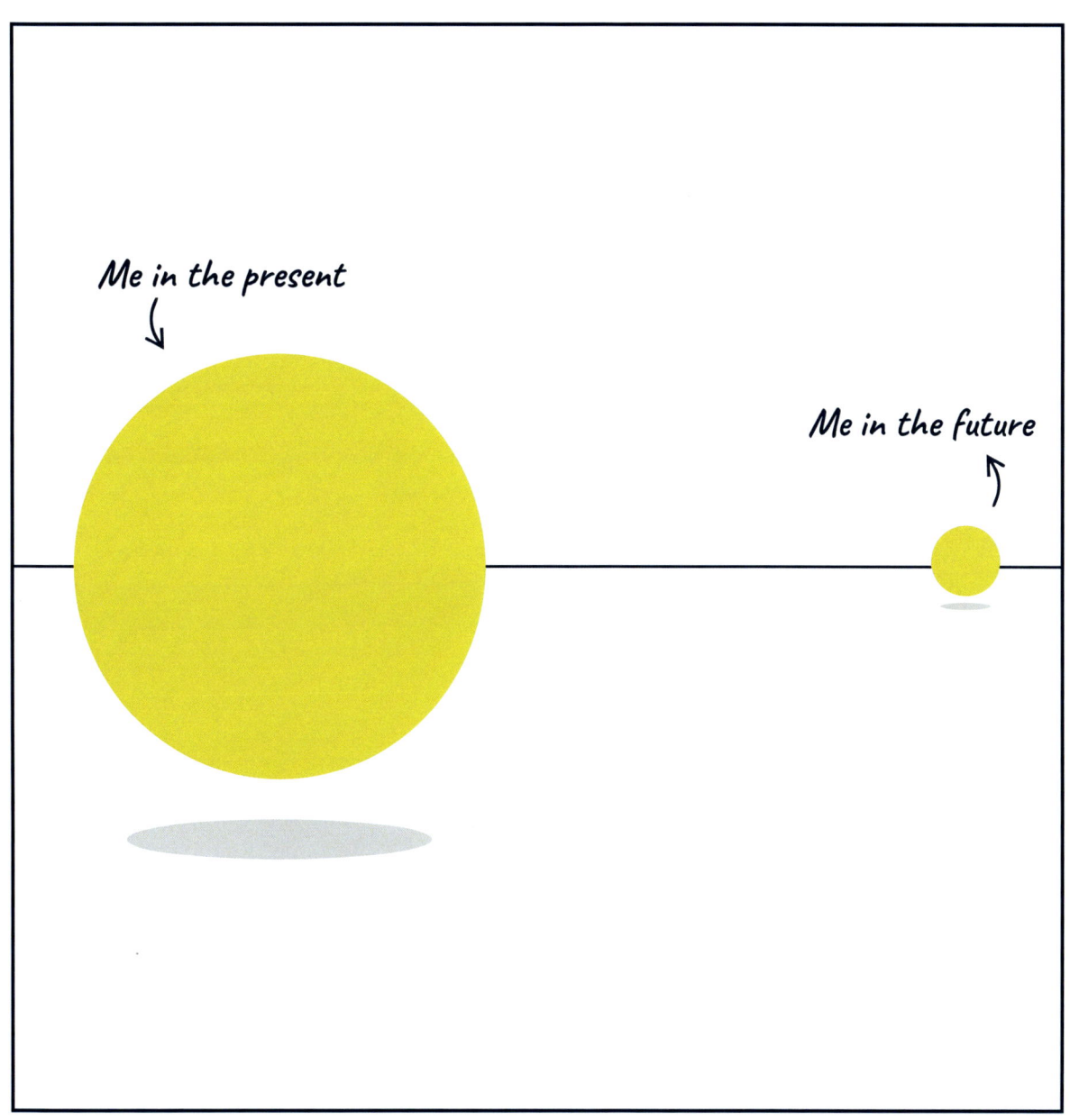

PHASE NINE: WHAT NEXT

Activities to help maintain momentum and growth.

―

Negative

~~It's the end of **the** road~~

~~I've reached the top of **the** mountain~~

~~The train has arrived at **its** destination~~

Positive

*It's the end of **this** road*

*I've reached the top of **this** mountain*

*This train has arrived at **this** destination*

PHASE NINE: WHAT NEXT

GOALS

ACTIVITY 9.1

Consider what you can accomplish, improve or change within the next five years.

Personal goals

| Learn First Aid | Learn Conversational Vietnamese | Become an author | Visit friends In America |

Professional goals

| Self employed, master of my own time | Establish a second income | | |

Family goals

| New Home | More travel | | |

Try sticky notes on a wall ↗

PHASE NINE: WHAT NEXT

DESIRES

ACTIVITY 9.2

Like a bucket list, think about all the cool things you want to experience.

Don't worry about how crazy or unrealistic they might be!

Write down all the cool things you're like to experience

A long and healthy life	Watch Child get married	Explore Vietnam with Son	Travel Europe with Wife

Try *sticky notes* on a wall or a *spreadsheet*

Write down all the cool things you're like to experience
Enjoy a long and healthy retirement
Have fun with my grandchildren
Return to Thailand and to Italy
Hiking and camping under the stars with my children
Become self-employed and financially stable to have freedom to be master of my own time and work from anywhere

PHASE NINE: WHAT NEXT

CONCERNS

ACTIVITY 9.3

Think about what keeps you up at night. What would address any concerns you may have and help to provide you with more peace of mind?

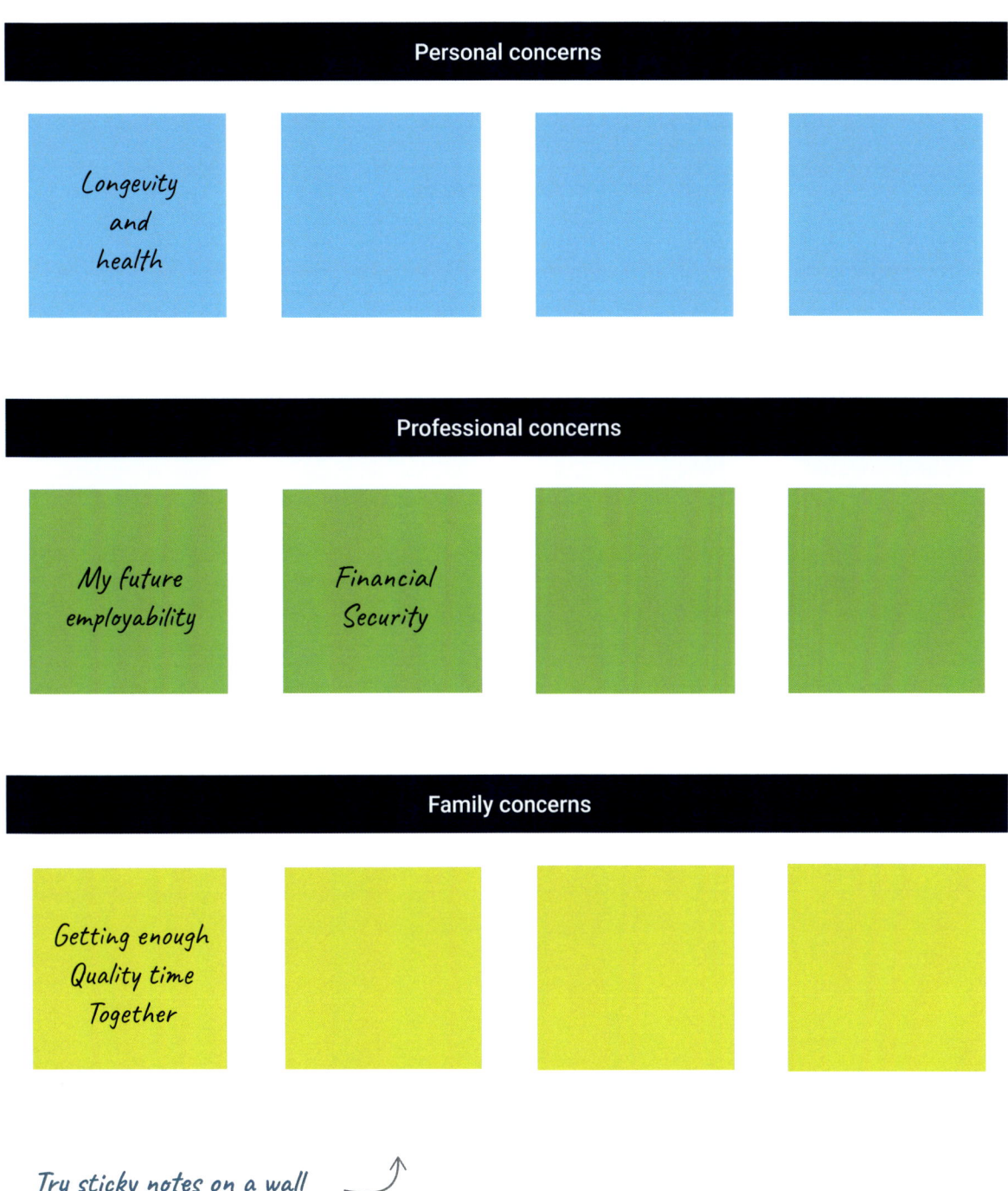

Try sticky notes on a wall

PHASE TEN:

EXPERIENCE

———

A single step (action) could lead to more steps (progress), a leap (an achievement) or a stumble (learning). Even when walking in circles, you're gaining a deeper understanding of your situation and exercising your potential to make progress.

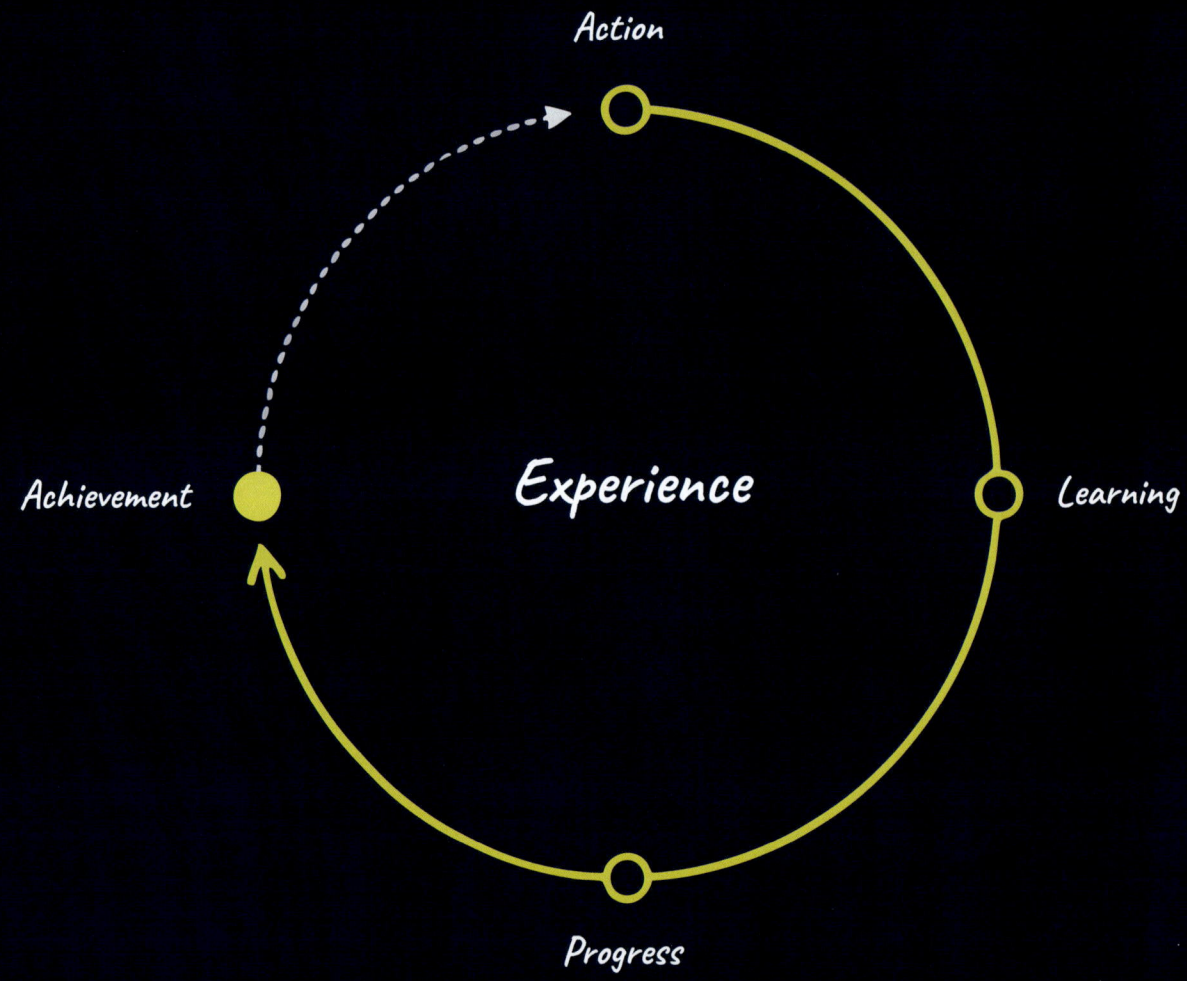

EXPERIENCE

Believing in yourself and proactively taking steps to improve your situation, helps you gain the experience and momentum needed to discover your purpose and achieve your potential. Succeed or fail, know that you're unique, one of a kind and that you've tried your best, and your best will improve with every step.

1. **Action**

    A step could lead to another step, forming a direction that can become purpose.

    What might help:

    - Go beyond your comfort zones, and broaden your horizon with challenging things.
    - Make changes to your behaviour to see changes in your situation.
    - Do more of what you enjoy and what makes you happy.
    - Embrace problems as opportunities and challenges to overcome.
    - Invest in your health, well-being and fitness to have the stamina to make a change and the longevity to enjoy it.

2. **Learning**

    A step could lead to a stumble, increasing your awareness and understanding of what's possible.

    What might help:

    - Learn from the experience of others. You're not alone; others travel with you, around you, and alongside you.
    - When yesterday didn't work out as expected, the unexpected can surprise you today and tomorrow.
    - Stay positive and focus on what's going well. Invest in yourself, even when others don't appreciate or support you.
    - Consider viewing a missed opportunity as a blessing in disguise.
    - Failure is an opportunity to learn something about yourself, such as what you value and what you might improve.

3. **Progress**

    A step could lead to walking, running, and great strides towards your goals.

    What might help:
    - Practice makes perfect and hard work pays off.
    - Gravitate towards positive situations and focus on what can be done rather than what can't by doing more of what works or feels good and less of what doesn't.
    - Avoid the pull of disruptive influences and behaviours that hinder progress.
    - When delays and setbacks occur, embrace the unexpected time as an opportunity to practice and refine your approach.
    - Gain new skills or abilities that will increase your chances of success.

4. **Achievement**

    A step could lead to a jump or a leap that lands you where you want to be or somewhere better than expected.

    What might help:
    - Explore and expand your horizons to unlock opportunities and potential.
    - Extend your connections for perspective and companionship.
    - Improve your environment for inspiration and enlightenment.
    - Evolve your circumstances for a better quality of life.

FINAL THOUGHTS

I hope this book helps you navigate from one situation to another to achieve a positive experience or perspective. Like any journey, there might be bumps, turbulence and discomfort depending on how you travel.

Growth isn't always easy, and can take time, effort and commitment where growing pains can come and go.

Don't wait for motivation or the right time to begin your journey. Motivation will likely come from what is unlocked when taking positive actions to invest in yourself. Try something different, make it a daily habit and see what happens.

You've surprised yourself before, and you can surprise yourself again.

ABOUT THE AUTHOR

Carl Hattley is an enthusiastic and energetic Design Leader with over 20 years of experience in driving and creating purposeful digital experiences for corporations and institutions across the globe that specialise in e-commerce, education, entertainment, energy and travel.

As a Leader, Carl's superpower is empathy for those he works with and supports. He encourages a collaborative and equitable environment where individuals feel understood, appreciated, inspired and empowered to thrive without fear of failure.

In this book, Carl combines techniques he evolved as a designer/manager with coping mechanisms he created to overcome Dyslexia, to arrive at frameworks and methodology that helped process information and navigate complex situations by framing problems, mapping opportunities and setting goals to drive positive outcomes in his career and personal life.

Website: http://chattleyworks.com/